THE EVIL WITHIN THEM

Written by

Michael Perry Allen

Introduction:

The Evil Within Them

From childhood to adult status. We all engage in both temporary and long-term meaningful and meaningless relationships. These encounters build character and knowledge you cannot obtain from reading a novel. One such novel title should read, '*How to Date After a Divorce.*'

This journey turned out to be more difficult than I expected.

Finding a significant and compatible partner was, nonetheless, an uphill battle, filled with, emotional highs and lows. The expensive rollercoaster ride with way too many curves to throw you off track in an instant. My experience with dating proved to be a learning experience more than the goal to find the perfect relationship.

I have embraced love, unloved, hated, cursed, hit, kicked, and left for another lover several times with, one dating experience so terrible, I was held captive inside her house, unable to leave without police protection.

With that said, I have embraced love but never felt I was "IN LOVE" with anyone for any length of time.

With each romance I felt comfortable, only to have that comfort eventually tarnished. Easy as I am on the eyes, a taller man than most with a physique and stature that seemed irresistible to pass up. I have continued to exercise at home or at the gym to stay physically fit. Thus, I was a target for the traits of a person with personality disorder. I have a charming southern personality and intellectual capacity to converse with anyone on a level of topics brought up in conversations.

Life has been good so far. The only exception is when I became so distraught with depression from my last relationship, I nearly took my life.

I am now 69 years old, with a determination to educate myself how evil people use manipulation to access, captivate and gain total control over others. How a narcissist chooses you for their personnel gain.. Playing a devious game with your emotions only to discard you like a used dishrag.

You are their source to perform multiple tasks and favors you have the skill to perform. Spend your money like it was theirs to begin with, while they never care for you in the first place. They have a plan already set in motion, and you are the expendable source needed to enrich their goals.

I realized I had been systematically engaged in manipulation tactics, I never imagined possible from a woman I deeply loved. I was the source for a professional narcissist.

I needed answers to critical issues lingering in my head from the first woman I thought I loved in high school in 1973 to the one person I trusted to be my soulmate for life.

I found the answers to my experiences with the women I have written about in this book. Extensive research into personality disorders provided clarity in understanding what happened and how it happened as it eventually provided acceptance of the evil acts they inflicted on me. The closure needed to move one with my life.

The complexity of the research could not have been, absorbed, or understood completely without the help of a professional therapist who I will call "Lisa."

My story, in my own words, from my life.

TABLE OF CONTENTS

The Evil Within Them

LCCN: TX 9-488-838

ISBN: 979-8-218-71739-1

Copyright 2024 by Michael Perry Allen

The Evil Within Them

Session One

Lisa was a short woman of an age older than me with a full head of chestnut brown hair flowing out and down her shoulders. Small rimmed glasses that fit her personality perfectly. It was obvious she had a booster in her seat to lift her small frame up from the chair to appear normal sized as she sat at her desk directly across from me with her arms firmly resting on the desk, fingers laced together. I was nervous the moment I walked in. The chair in front of her desk was an old wooden frame with the seat carved just perfectly for my cheeks to settle in. It was noticeably warm from the earlier client who must have been hot natured.

Lisa: "What brings you in today? Mr. Allen, is it? Would you prefer I call you Mike, Michael, or the more professional address?"

Michael will be fine.

The Evil Within Them

Lisa: "I have your file in front of me with the questionnaire you filled out. Aside from that please tell me a little about yourself and why you believe you need a therapist."

"I assume you do not need my entire life history from birth so I will forgo all that information and begin with my current situation and why I am here in the first place. Will that work for you?"

Lisa: "Absolutely, but I need background information from your life to be able to understand you and what bothers you before I can try a diagnosis. You do understand this is in no way a quick fix. You have written down in your initial questionnaire information that needs addressing during our sessions.

"Sessions? You have pluralized the statement."

Lisa: "Yes, I have. For me to help you. You must commit to a series of sessions on a weekly or monthly basis. The VA is paying for the therapy, so you are not responsible for the costs currently."

"Yes. Yes of course, I do understand. I will begin with this. I have had relationship issues my entire life. The struggle I have is about finding the right person to embrace me for who I am and realize I have enough to offer that they do not need to move on to someone else."

Lisa: "You just mentioned, "Finding the right person?" Have you ever felt you had the right person in your life? You were married for 24 years. Have there been others before or afterward? What about this other issue of finding someone else? Did anyone cheat on you or move on quickly to another after a breakup?"

"That later statement is the core of my problems with women and supporting long term relationships. Marriage is a contract that will bind you to someone. But the others are free agents that will use and abuse at will. They have nothing to lose, or I should say gain from playing the field."

The Evil Within Them

Lisa: "Can you begin there and elaborate on when the first time this has happened to you?"

Silence filled the room as I began recalling the memories of my first love.

Lisa: "MICHAEL!"

"Sorry, my mind wondered off. I am back now."

"Lisa: Where did you go? I have been sitting here for a couple minutes while you went into thought about someone or something. What was it?"

"Sherrie. Her name was Sherrie. My first. Well, I thought it was my first love. It was 1973. High school lunchroom type romance. She was the most beautiful girl I knew at the time. Long blonde curly hair. We would meet daily in the lunchroom and have lunch. I

4

was thoroughly impressed by her hair and her ability to engage in discussions on any topic.

I drove an old 1960's model Volkswagen to East Bay high school in Gibsonton, Florida. We lived out in the country, so it was about thirty miles to the high school. I would pick her up on the way in that old red Volkswagen with a white racing strip across the hood.

My father owned a couple gas stations and was a fairly decent mechanic. The old car needed tweaking all the time to keep it running. It often broke down and Sherrie never said a word as we waited for my father to show up and fix it. Then off again to school."

Lisa: "Go on, tell me more about her. You are here to talk about you, and I am here to listen."

"I am not as comfortable with this therapy as you might think. Am I on the right track. This part of my life was a long time ago and it may not be significant information to address my current situation."

The Evil Within Them

Lisa: "Everything in your life has a piece of information that brings you to your current situation... Little bits of your timeline. Like connecting dots to a game. I need to know about you and your life as I can. So, tell me more about your experience with Sherrie. What happened to that relationship? Did you marry her? Was she your wife?"

Trauma occurs suddenly, while depression often stems from past experiences.

Lisa snaps her finger in my face, and I recover once again from wandering off to 1973 again.

"It was bellbottom pants and smoking cigarettes in the designated smoking area of the school. Sherrie always had cigarettes and a flip top lighter. We would share drags on one cigarette until it was gone. That encounter was all I needed. It was my Sherrie fix for the day. Just seeing her standing in front of me fulfilled me. She had those bellbottom pants hugging her hips without back pockets. To this day I do not know where she hid the bulky lighter and perfectly straight cigarette we smoked. Under all that blonde curly hair I suppose."

Lisa: "Did you see her outside of school? A movie or a walk in the park? You seem to have had a great relationship building up with her."

"Two years. Two full school years, No summers together. No contact outside of school. We were young. My parents struggled with financial stability. So, no money for dating. It was during our Junior and Seniors years of high school. I played football for the East Bay Indians. She would attend the Friday night games. I would look for her in the bleachers or pick her out of the crowd as she was walking the Track that encircled the field we were playing on. She always waved or came up to the security fence to say hello. We did not kiss or hug, nothing like that. I can look back now and assess she was kind and gentle with me. I think she just did not want to hurt me more than she did."

Lisa: "Wait. What did you say? Hurt you? How so?"

7

The Evil Within Them

Fingers SNAPPING again.

"I know, I pause often. I must search my memory for a moment to get the facts straight. So be patient with me. As I mentioned it was 1973, now I am up to1974. The year of my senior graduation year. We were still seeing each other daily. It was our routine. I picked her up for school. But now it was a different vehicle. The Volkswagen was gone for good and my father precured a 1966 Ford Mustang. You should have seen the smile on her face when I surprised her the morning, I drove up her driveway to pick her up.

Sherrie: "You have a MUSTANG! This is so cool."

"I opened the passenger door for her as I always did. Every morning, I was her chauffeur. She would get in and turn that beautiful head of hair back towards me and smile. That day she had a much larger smile. I felt so lucky to have her in my life.

8

The Evil Within Them

Although I had my ideas and comfort zone with her. It was not her idea of a relationship. I was just her source. She despised riding the bus. It was too traumatic for her. All the guys were hitting on her during the long ride to school. She saw me as a way out of that situation."

Lisa: "I see where you are going with your story, please continue."

"I thought nothing of it. It never dawned on me to be manipulated for her personnel gain. I provided a safety net for her life. In return I got attention. That was all. We never saw much of each other outside of high school. Looking back on the lunchtime meets I also provided a measure of safety for her. If my old car would not start in the morning. I missed picking her up. I would scramble to catch the bus at the end of our dirt driveway. No cell phones or internet communications back then. I would look for her when I got off the bus. Realizing later she would just stay home. Refusing to put herself in a position where she would endure intimidation or bullying while riding the bus to school."

9

The Evil Within Them

Lisa: "How so?"

"Look at me. I am a big guy. Nobody bothered her while we were sitting together. Looking back on those lunches, I realize now I am her bodyguard. She could eat lunch in peace and quiet. Very few guys tried for her attention while she was with me. Most guys would walk by our table and say Hi to her, but she hardly gave them a look or a wave with her hand to make them keep going. She always kept eye contact with me as she thwarted the best attempts for her attention. That was my solace. I thought she liked me more than them. I was her man. She always kept me close to her when we walked from the lunchroom to her classroom. Always asking if I would be there to walk her to her next class. I was always in trouble for being late to my own classes. My teachers asked why I was late for class. Although being on the star football team, notable district champions. The teachers just looked the other way instead of writing me up."

The Evil Within Them

Lisa: "You were on the football team? Gallantly providing protection from the bullies and potential suitors?"

"Yes."

"I was oblivious to the real reason she attached herself to me. There was no reason to believe she had other intentions. Back then, you do not hang around a boy in high school unless you have interest in him, that is how it was. I developed strong feelings for her."

Lisa: "I am hearing all the good you have to say about Sherrie, now tell me what troubled you about her. What happened between you two that was, not so pleasant? Did she betray your trust? You have described a relationship that should be picture-perfect, but you have more to tell me, don't you?"

"Yes, I do."

"We were finishing our senior year, and now the end of May 1974. The final weeks were closing in and honestly there was no need to even attend those final

11

days. For reasons I cannot recall, I stopped picking her up in the Mustang. I assumed her parents brought her to school. Although we were still meeting in the lunchroom, our smoking sessions also curtailed."

Lisa: "You left me again. Come back to me Michael. Do I need to snap my fingers?"

"No, you do not. I needed a moment to gather myself before continuing."

"Ok, I have it in my head now."

"The last day Sherrie attended school. Like clockwork she entered the lunchroom and sat across the table from me. Always across from me, never beside me like you would expect in a realistic relationship. I could see she was visibly upset; tears were forming on her cheeks. I at once asked if someone had bullied her?"

Sherrie: "No, not that at all. Michael, I have something I should tell you."

The Evil Within Them

"She then stood up, turned to walk away, then hesitated for me to step up beside her. This was our protocol. We began walking side by side like a normal day. Something was wrong, wrong that day."

"She slowed and turned to speak, not paying attention to the lunchroom furniture, she stumbled over a chair in her path, I caught her in my arms to break her fall. She was lighter than I had expected. Quickly and easily, I embraced her frame as I helped her right herself.

The first time in two years, Sherrie wrapped her arms around me in full embrace, holding me tight, her head buried into my shoulder. I could feel her body sobbing, gasping for air. I can still remember the smell of lavender in her hair.

Her father owned a profitable trucking company. So, it was no surprise his daughter had the best of everything available to her. Salty tears flowed down her face and wet my jersey. I could feel her warm breath begin to whisper in my ear the words I never wanted to hear."

Sherrie: "Michael, I am pregnant."

The Evil Within Them

Lisa: "Oh My! You must have been devastated?"

"You have no idea how that day changed my perspective on relationships. The entire summer of 1974 was difficult for me to accept. The depression set in. The Gas embargo was taking profound effects on the U.S. economy. There were no jobs for young people or anyone for that matter.

My father had lost his job, and my mother was the only bread winner in the family. One day my father sat me down and suggested I join the U.S. Army."

"The decision to join the armed services was an easy one. I needed to get out of town and start a new life."

Lisa: "As I see it. Sherrie was using you for protection only. You were her security blanket. As you know, she did not have the same feelings you had for her. She let you believe she did. This is why she

14

struggled to convey there was a real boyfriend outside the school atmosphere. She could not come to terms with her choice in life. Do you see this now?"

"I reflect on the timeline of my life. Being young, I unwillingly let her control the situation. I am not sure if she was being purposefully devious or evil, she had a need to manipulate me for her own safety. I provided a service to control sanity in what I assumed was from an insane educational system she had to attend or a safe escape from family problems.

I forgave her. Although I never saw her again to tell her my thoughts.

"I NEVER SPOKE TO HER AGAIN!"

"I will add to that statement. Never speaking to her again was her choice. I adored her and would have happily stayed connected with her. She chose to disappear from my life. I assume she left with the man she had the intimate relationships with or to have the baby somewhere out of wedlock. I will never know that answer."

The Evil Within Them

Lisa: "Let me write all this down in your file for now. This initial session is at an end for today, our time is up. When are you available to return? We need to continue to address the rest of your experiences. I appreciate your open response to the questioning."

"Fine with me. I have more episodes to-as they say, "get off my chest." Next Month, same date and time? Oh! By the way. How long do you think I will need therapy? One final question before I go. What are your thoughts about me?"

Lisa: "There is no way I can answer you honestly with only one session completed. I will need to analyze more information to conclude a diagnosis. But from this first session I believe you have built a depression-based opinion on the circumstances you had to deal with.

"Ok, I will return with more information on the rest of them."

The Evil Within Them

Lisa: "The rest of them? Never mind for now. I will set a reminder to have the staff text you an appointment reminder next month. See you next time."

The Evil Within Them

Session Two

Entering the waiting room of Lisa's office. I take a seat on a worn-out leather couch from a by gone era. I keep wondering about the number of people who have sat here waiting for their session to start. Therapy for me was never a needed possibility. I stand strong and portray myself with dignity and authority. I am an analytical thinker with situational awareness. This mindset has been an asset to my life. Helping individuals and corporations solve issues they cannot. Whether it is in production, construction, or mechanical nature, every company I work for looks to engage my opinion on use of space for production to help them. The companies I have personally owned myself are still operational.

My motto is: "I know how to put round pegs in square holes."

"I just cannot figure out how to keep a relationship."

The Evil Within Them

Lisa: "Good afternoon, Michael. Please take a seat, my last client just left so the old chair has not had time to cool down."

"I noticed at our last meeting. You must get your clients all heated up in here?"

Lisa: "Surely you are making a pun. My clients often arrive in a heightened state, and I focus on helping them feel more at ease before the session concludes. What are your thoughts from our last session? Have you reflected on our last session and the experience enough to accept that part of your life?"

"That chapter with Sherrie as the character left me a long time ago. The memories may remain locked away forever. My mind is not like a computer hard drive, there is no way to erase the stored material in it."

Lisa: "Pretty amazing to hear a client say that. Most people do not have the ability to rationalize their memories in such a way. I would not have a profession if they did?"

Laughter fills the room for a moment as we both knowingly receive the information is too funny not to laugh about.

Lisa: "Ok then, let us begin our session. What would you like to discuss today? Is today a who would you like to discuss?"

Lisa snaps her fingers together; I had already lapsed into another one of my time zones. I look up to her gazing eyes staring at me. Her eyebrows momentarily rise, signifying questionability. I realize time is important as she has entered her professional portal and needed me to get on with my story.

"I am not sure where to begin, Lisa? To use a metaphor, I will say, "this is outside of my box." So, to speak.

The Evil Within Them

Lisa: "I always recommend my clients try to pick up where you left off from our last session. Can you recall your memory of those last statements you made?"

"Yes, I can. My father suggested joining Armed Services. He was in the Airforce for 20 years, SAC Command. Hardly ever saw the man until he retired. Then I often wish he had not, but he was able to pass on one good characteristic of himself. The love for the outdoors. He was always a real country boy, born and raised in a wooden shack in the middle of a tobacco field. That old shack of the house with a couple of bedrooms and a kitchen, single wooden slats for exterior walls, not a single piece of insulation in the walls or ceiling."

Lisa: "Do you want to share any traumatic experiences from your time in the service during this session? What did you do in the Army?"

"My father was the same as I am today, I will not discuss my time in the service to anyone. I will tell you this and only this bit of information. I did things that made most grown men crawl into a fetal position and cry like a baby and that is all I will divulge to you. The rest will stay locked in memory forever. It is the only way I can emotionally cope with that time."

Lisa: "I can agree with you on that point." I will note, not to ask again."

I make eye contact with Lisa, as I pause to allow her to digest what I said. She finishes her thoughts.

Lisa: "I understand your position. If your performance is not upsetting to you, then let those memories stay locked away where they are."

"Thank you, I will leave that subject for another day. I need to discuss my issues with relationship failures."

23

The Evil Within Them

Lisa: "Let us move forward to the time after your discharge. What did you do when you came back home? Any specific relationship you would like to discuss?"

"I had brief encounters while I attended night classes to become an electrician with the I.B.E.W. I was too busy working during the day and attending the trade school at night. Nothing lasted more than a few weeks at most. There was not enough time to develop a long-term bond. If I were not at work or school, I would go to my brother-in-law's garage to help build his dirt track racecar on the weekends."

Lisa: "How did you meet your wife?

"One apprentice assignment to an electrical contractor, we were to renovate a local bank. That is where I was, introduced to the woman I married."

The Evil Within Them

Lisa: "Oh yes, I remember you mentioned one marriage in your paperwork. Tell me about that. You wrote it lasted 24 years. How did that end?"

"How do I express all that happened in that duration of time into one session? It is impossible."

Lisa: "There is no requirement to compress the years into an hour session. We can stretch this out in segments of your life, like five to ten years at a time. Therapy is more about me understanding the trouble you have with relationships. Only then can I provide you with help and answers to the questions you might have. It is reasonable to assess whether you have selected to be in that seat in front of me."

"Am I correct?"

"Michal, I am about to snap my fingers again!"

"Sorry, I drifted off to 1981 working on the bank."

The Evil Within Them

Lisa: "Go on."

"Here is a condensed version. Marriage started off ok. She was married to an abuser when I met her. He punched her in the stomach at six months of pregnancy with their child in hopes of forcing a miscarriage. She had the child anyway. With her divorce from him settled, we got married. Although She was great to be with. I needed to prove to myself and her girlfriends I could settle down and be a good man to her and her son. The trash talk from other bank females was, to say the least-ugly at times. Mostly disgruntled married women anyway."

"I will add her son became the lone factor in the dismantling of our relationship together."

Lisa: "Can you elaborate on the aspect of the son being the sole problem in your relationship? It sounds like you and your wife were in an ok relationship, and he caused problems between you and her? So, correct me if I am wrong. You did not have relationship issues with her? Was it the stepson you had a problem with?"

The Evil Within Them

"I would not put in the terms of "I" had a problem with him. It was more of him having a problem with "me," or any man having a relationship with his mom. He has proven that statement enough times over the years we were together including her relationships after we received our separation.

I can conclude she was the only woman I did not have personnel issue with that I felt would have caused a dysfunctional environment where we needed to part ways over."

Lisa: "Then what was it?"

"Every problem we had in our relationship together was, directly connected by her son. Everything that boy did was ignored. He started trouble in school, trouble holding job, He would steal, lie, cheat, buy drugs and never pay the dealers, he was constantly in trouble with the law, arrested twenty-eight separate times. Finally getting, sentenced to a year and a half in a correctional institute for grand theft. She visited him at the facility every Sunday, sending thousands and thousands of dollars to his cooper trust fund to pay off the other inmates to keep him from being, assaulted on the inside."

"Hold those thoughts, I need a break. Do Not Snap your fingers, LISA!"

Lisa: "Take a moment, I will patiently await your return."

Regaining my composure, making eye contact with Lisa to signal I am ready.

Lisa asks.

Lisa: "If you are ready to continue? I have a question before we begin."

"Yes, what is your question?"

The Evil Within Them

Lisa: "It is more of an observation to your last statement than a question but here goes. In your questionnaire you wrote down and referenced you were seeking answers to failed relationships, and you considered you were to blame for them. Listening to you since the beginning of our sessions. I find a pattern of abuse in marriage you do not fully understand the effect it has on your self-esteem.

That mental abuse is not your fault. The case here is to understand, you were the recipient of a pattern connected to a personality disorder. Activities by an individual, albeit connected to you with relationships or the marital bond with your wife, show an evil within that person that inflicted this traumatic experience on you. This action is no fault of your own doing. It is all of them."

"Do you understand what I just said, Michael?"

"I can comprehend what you are saying."

Lisa: "Good, are you ready to continue with your story?"

29

The Evil Within Them

"There is so much to this chapter of my life, I find it difficult to begin, and I may jump around with timelines as we progress in our sessions. So, bear with me, not all will be pleasant to understand.

You have listened to how I managed him during his younger years. Her support of his shenanigans continues through his life."

Lisa: "Are you Irish?"

"Family tree has been, traced back to the old country. There are branches to my family tree, no one knows the whole picture. My sister knows more about our genealogy than I do. I am just a leaf on the family tree somewhere at the top. With the aid of a good strong wind, erased off the tree for good."

Lisa: "Elaborate on that for me, will you? It will give me insight to who I am sharing a conversation with."

The Evil Within Them

"My sister and mother were into genealogy. Tracing our history from the old country to the new world. Some ancestors were on the three ships from Spain. Forward from that to the civil war era, one of my ancestors was General Lee's first man at Appomattox when he surrendered to General Ulysees Grant. Further on from the civil war I have another relative Elisiah Tyler who became an honored businessperson in South Carolina after the Civil War. They have named a bridge in Horry County South Carolina with his namesake. Before the Civil War began there was one more famous notable fellow in my family history. I am a direct relation to the tenth President of the United States, President John Tyler. So, I have a blue-ribbon pedigree to wave in front of people."

Lisa: "Wow, which is impressive. Although I have a small pedigree of mutts in my family. I see where your intellect comes from."

"Thank-you Lisa, flattery will get you everywhere."

The Evil Within Them

Lisa: "Although impressive to hear we have ventured off path. Please tell me more about your tenure of marriage."

"As I mention the stories get better, or should I refer to it as getting worse. Yes, I think the word "worse" better describes what you will hear from me. When my wife filed for divorce from her first husband, her ex-husband's mother had a grudge against my wife for leaving the brutal marriage.

"I do believe her ex, told his mother a completely different version of the truth. Understanding her love for own her son, she was notably angry at my wife for leaving the relationship and started a campaign of aggressive behavior towards us for living together."

Thinking it would cause us discomfort by calling our home phone on a regular basis. We would answer but no one would say anything in return. Those were the days when a phone system did not have caller I.D. Constant, relentless calling.

I knew it had to be her ex-mother in-law. One day I had enough of it. I decided the next time the phone rang and instead of answering cordially, I began an onslaught of verbal abuse an old sailor would be proud of. The caller hung up, and within an hour the mother-in-law called back."

This time she asked, "How did I know it was her on the line?"

Lisa: "You called her out." How did she respond to that?"

"She quit the harassing calls. Eventually after a couple of years she settled down and accepted our relationship together. We actually became friends later on."

"Unfortunately, that was not the end of it, and we decided a change of venue was necessary. I got a job out of state, and we moved to Aiken, South Carolina from Florida fleeing the ex-husband and his dysfunctional, uncooperative band of family members. We thought we were in a place they knew nothing about. It turns out the stepson's grandmother grew up in Aiken, South Carolina. Her local nickname was Stinky, I cannot recall why."

The Evil Within Them

"Fast forward to the start of my business career as an electrical contractor. From the point of conception of informing my wife of my goal to be the best electrical contractor in the South, I began enduring the verbal abuse of how worthless I had become to her, adding insult to the mix of abuse, during one of her verbal assaults launched against my character, she informed me I was nothing and never going to make it as a businessman."

That was the moment I set course to prove her wrong. I built a highly respected business covering three states with millions in contracts signed each year. I become a highly respected electrical contractor, employing hundreds of men and women."

Lisa: "How did she react to all of that success?"

"Quite literally that woman never praised or thanked me, not once in 17 years of owning the business. I will say she helped spend every dime of money she could get access too. She wanted for nothing during its operating years.

The Evil Within Them

As for the stepson I graciously tried to get him involved in the business. Every opportunity I laid out for him, he would work for a noticeably brief period, then he would quit the job, take the paycheck he earned then disappear looking for drugs. This became his motus-operandi for the rest of his working life as an adult."

Lisa: What role did your wife have in the discipline of this boy? Did she council him, try to discourage this activity in any way?"

"What discipline, discourage? Every time he was in trouble, from the day he was born. She took him out to a store and bought him a new outfit or new shoes. She praised and rewarded his evil behavior or criminal activities. Leading him to believe his activity was, guaranteed to receive recognition in some form."

Lisa: "I am getting a clear understanding why you are here. Please continue."

35

The Evil Within Them

"I feel like I need a cigarette and a bourbon at the moment."

Lisa: "Wait I have read your file. You have not shown any use of tobacco of alcohol currently."

"I do not smoke or drink. That was a pressure release statement."

Lisa: "I see. Wait, where are you going?"

"I must stand up. That old wooden chair is hurting my butt cheeks."

Lisa: "Can I get you a pillow to sit on?"

"No. You could spend a part of my session payments and get a more comfortable chair for my next visit. That would be a nice gesture, anyway I thought you therapists had couches for your clients to lay on while you took notes. Where is the couch?"

The Evil Within Them

"I need a couch in here Lisa."

Lisa: "Sorry there is no couch. Although I will confess, everyone asks about the missing couch."

"I might need add you to my list of abusive females I have met in my life. Making me sit on that chair for an hour would qualify you for the list. As for the couch, my advice is to listen to your clients."

Lisa: "I am the therapists, Michael! I give the advice in here."

"Touche,' although a couch."

Lisa interrupts my verbal thoughts.

Lisa: "I think this will conclude our session for today. Do you have any questions for me before we set a date for our next meeting?

The Evil Within Them

"I suppose I do, need to ask once again for your opinion of the therapy sessions so far. Two sessions should offer insight whether I am crazy or not."

Lisa: "Have you read the book, Catch 22?"

"Matter of fact I have."

Lisa: "Then you know the answer to your question." See you next month. Since you are still standing you can go ahead and see your way out.

"Well, ok then. See you next month.

Session Three

I entered the room to greet Lisa, my therapist. She was standing next to her desk with a brilliant smile. Looking around I found new décor. The old wooden chair had been replaced with a more modern soft cushioned chair. Close to the wall I notice a chase lounge replacing an open bare wall. Where a credenza and lamp once stood alone.

Lisa's desk, including filing cabinets, also upgraded from institutional steel grade to a pleasant wood grain finish. The room had a comfortable feeling in it. She was proud of her achievement in modernizing her office space.

I could not help but compliment her on the change in décor. Hearing my voice with the words she waited to hear, her lips formed a beautiful smile. I could tell Lisa needed to hear those words from me. For a moment I filled the therapeutic hunger she desperately needed from me.

Lisa: "Shall we sit, or would you prefer I sit in the chair, and you stretch out on the chase lounge? You now have options Michael."

39

The Evil Within Them

"I think we can continue the session sitting across from each other at the desk if you do not mind."

Lisa: "Perfect. How does the seat feel to you when sitting in the chair?"

"Like a used car salesperson once said to me. Every car has a seat, and there is a butt for every seat cushion. I am good."

Lisa: "Good to know. I will remember that for days to come. Now tell me more about the later days of your marriage and the stepson."

"You should get a fresh notepad, a new pen to write everything I am about to tell you. Otherwise, you might run out of ink. I mentioned in the earlier sessions. The number of times her son was arrested. Included in those years of trouble with the law, the schools he attended added to his history of evil behavior.

The Evil Within Them

Lisa: "Why the reference to evil in his behavior?"

His entire childhood was engulfed in turmoil. Once he became a legal adult, he exhibited a comprehensive, calculated, thoroughly planned intention to do harm to people, jobs, structures, automobiles, including verbal life-threatening assault to anyone he deemed to having authority to correct him or a threat to his lifestyle in some way. He conducted this aggressive behavior with premeditative precision. That is the mindset of an evil person whose actions were the result of un-provoked behavior, not reactive behavior derived from a circumstance or retaliatory need to get back at someone. I will add this to that last statement; it did not matter there was never a rhyme or reason anyone could point out a justification as to why he picked an individual specific target, he did what he did to them."

Lisa: "Can you provide a few instances of this calculated behavior?"

The Evil Within Them

"I mentioned, you may need that extra pen. I recall a time when he was visiting his grandparents for a
weekend. They had no understanding as neither of us
the gravity of his behavior at that age of 8 or 9 years
old.

After he returned to us from the weekend stay.
Everyone went back to normal living. We went back to
work, and the boy returned to school. The timeline I
mentioned may be incomplete, but I am recalling dec-
ades of memory.

My wife received a call from the grandmother
of the ex-husband. She began to explain how she had
been robbed of her jewelry right out from under her
nose. A lengthy conversation ensued to describe that
she had left her door unlocked and she was distraught
over when someone entered her home and took all her
expensive jewelry, which included diamond necklaces
and bracelets. The Police were there and fully involved
in investigating the crime.

Weeks forward from reporting the crime. The
school hosted a parent teacher night for family members
with the students to show off their classwork and the
atmosphere of the classroom. I did not attend because I

was the stepdad. His real father and stepmother attended."

"His Father sat at his son's desk. He reached into the cubby of the desk, looking for his son's school paperwork; instead of school papers, he retrieved a small brown paper bag filled with his mother's expensive jewelry. The monetary value was in the thousands. The boy had somehow systematically figured out how to enter his grandmother's bedroom with a paper bag to steal the diamond jewelry without her or anyone's knowledge. He then took it to his classroom that next week to hide it at his desk. No explanation was given for this action. He refused to answer interrogations from his father or police when they were, notified of the jewelry's retrieval."

Lisa: "Was he punished for this? I do not condone corporal punishment, but was any form of punishment administered upon him by any family member?"

"Not a single word from any family member. Nothing, no administering disciplinary actions to correct his behavior, no teaching of right and wrong. In

43

fact, his mother, my wife, took him to a clothing store and bought him a new outfit for his return to school the next day. He learned that his actions gained rewards instead of punishment."

"That was the beginning of the evil monster he became."

Lisa: "I assure you kids do things like this all the time. I see parents who have struggled with children taking possession of personal items from their parents innocently. Do you think it was a show and telling event that moved him to take the items from his grandmother's bedroom?"

"At the time, yes, we covered that scenario. Looking back at his history now. No, not at all. He knew where the jewelry could be found by watching his grandmother remove it and store it away. He then calculated in detail how and when the opportunity presented itself to enter the room with stealth precision to remove the items from her dresser drawer. Then he placed the box back in the drawer, in the exact position he found it. Preventing his grandmother from suspecting anything was wrong until she needed the jewelry again. He had an ability to calculate the action of taking of the jewelry along with replacing the jewelry box back in the drawer in the exact same position to avoid suspicion by his grandmother.

Lisa: "Amazing. You are positive he did this at that age with clear intentions to steal the items and not for any other intent?

"I understand your position as a therapist to get me to see another side to his behavior as an innocent child doing childish activities. I can assure you at the end of our sessions you will agree with me this boy was not a normal child."

Lisa: "While I am writing this down in my notes, can you reflect on more behavior you wish to share? If you take too long, I will snap my fingers."

"I am beginning to appreciate your candid response to my drifting off. So, it is, I will begin again

45

The Evil Within Them

with more of the story. The school began calling us to detail the boys' daily activities or I should mention, his lack of participation to complete daily assignments.

We asked for suggestions on how we could help achieve the goals the curriculum set during the day. The response from his teacher was a simple observation. He is easily distracted by others, and he will not listen to instructions.

Our response was. How can we help to ensure he gets the classwork completed? After a lengthy discussion we all agreed to have the teacher write down the assignments on a piece of paper or a small notebook. We eventually agreed, we would buy a notepad to send to school with him. The teacher would then write the required homework assignment in the notebook to include which study book is, referenced with pages he was to read and the perform the required self-test at the end of the chapters and return the work the next day for grading."

Lisa: "Interesting concept. How did that plan work out?"

The Evil Within Them

"The teacher was as concerned about his early education as we were. With the plan in place. The boy would come home from school with the assignment written in the notebook by his teacher, then my wife would spend time helping him begin with the correct book and pages. For the first week this plan was on track and was working flawlessly."

"One day I happened to be home from work early. My wife called me into her son's bedroom to discuss a concern about his homework assignment. She showed me the notepad where the teacher had written the required assignment. I began asking questions to figure out what was wrong. I then asked to see the notebook the teacher wrote his assignments in."

Lisa: "You are pausing. Why?"

"I checked the notepad to confirm the assigned task the teacher wrote down. I could see where she wrote down a single assignment for homework that night, further investigating I realized the teacher used a pencil to write the assignments in the notepad. It appeared to me the rest of the scheduled work had been erased, leaving only one assignment to be completed.

The boy had used an eraser to omit the other assignments written in the notebook. He was so devious at an early age. Using a tactic to deceive his mom into believing he had one homework task and systematically erased the other assignments written in pencil by the teacher. He was around ten years old at that time."

Lisa: "That does sound apprehensive to me. I cannot imagine his mind being that advanced at that age to process such cunning thoughts and to implement such a plan to perfection."

"The iceberg is always bigger underneath. There is much more to him than I have mentioned. Of course, my wife never blamed his lack of attention on him, she always directed the blame on the public school system."

He was smarter than regular children his age. We addressed the issue by applying for admittance to a private academy. Hoping his attendance at a quality education facility will help him succeed. To no avail it did not last a full calendar school year. The school's Headmaster called us in to his office to inform us her son was being at once removed from classes and their curriculum. My wife tried in vain to get this man to change his mind, citing her son was a good person and needed to still be in class.

The school's Headmaster cut her off as he informed her, her son had a thirty average aptitude score, and this establishment would not accept his lack of interest in his education. We took him home that day and enrolled him back in the public school system the next day."

Lisa: "Wow, which painted a pretty picture for me. Excuse me a moment, I am writing as fast as I can."

"Once again, no immediate punishment was, administered. Just another rewarding trip to the clothing store for a new outfit."

"One morning my wife was sick and could not get out of bed. I began the task of preparing him for school. Getting clothes laid out and I picked out his shoes. The outfit was ok, but he informed me the shoes I selected did not match his outfit and refused to wear them. That statement usually comes from an adult female who selectively matches her attire. I was, taken back by his request to change the color of his shoes to match the outfit. As I looked for the proper shoes, I stood gazing at the number of shoes in the closet my wife had bought him."

Lisa: "You are saying at that young age he had the thought process to dress himself in matching attire?"

"Amazing but true. My wife took full credit for his appearance. That protocol of having new, clean, scuff free shoes and clothing became his modus operandi for the rest of his life. Except for the time of his imprisonment. The other inmates just stole his shoes or other garments from him. He received a taste of his own medicine for a while. He looked good in orange."

The Evil Within Them

Lisa: "You are kidding me, right? Did the time he served for a crime deter him in any way when he was, released?"

"Deter him, Oh No, not at all. He was a legal adult at the time of his release. Days later we received another call from the law enforcement that he was, picked up for driving without a license and in possession of paraphernalia, held for the weekend until a judge could set bond. We would bail him out quite often. Then we just stopped bailing him out."

Lisa: Why?"

"He would call relentlessly asking us to bail him out. We asked him to stop getting in trouble because the bail money was drying up for him."

Lisa: "How did he respond to telling him about the bail money?"

"Oh, he responded all right. He informed us he did not care if we stopped posting bail. Jail was not so bad, and the county would eventually let him out on a PR bond eventually. So, it did not make sense for us to pay out any more money. He said stop doing it if you do not have the money."

"Since that time when we began refusing bail money. The County detention center started letting him out on a P.R. bond."

Lisa: "I am not familiar with that terminology so, please provide descriptive information."

"A- P.R. Bond is short for, Personnel reconnaissance. They just get tired of providing tax dollars to houses and feed them. Every Monday morning, the County detention center would let the weekenders walk out the front door without bail. Again, no punishment administered by the authorities who locked him up or his mother. He quickly learned, he could now up his game of evil agenda's."

The Evil Within Them

Lisa: "I am speechless now. Please continue."

"During the year and a half, he spent incarcerated in Turbeville Correctional facility My wife would visit him every Sunday."

Lisa: "You mentioned that earlier. Is there more to that story you need to tell me?"

"Years have passed since all of this has happened; it will take several sessions to tie it all together.

My wife's mother had already passed away a year earlier and now her father has passed away. I was in Ohio with her taking care of his affairs. His will now read to both daughters by his lawyer. His assets and money were left to four charities. The rest of his savings account indicated a distribution to her and her sister. It was a hefty sum of money to inherit. I remember each of them received a little over $80,000.00.

Lisa: "How is that relevant to the last statements?"

The Evil Within Them

"My wife sent close to 60% of her inheritance to that correctional facility for his cooper trust funding during his incarceration."

Lisa: "No way!'

"Yes. Unbelievable, isn't it?"

Lisa: "Yes, it is. My question is how did you cope with all this?"

"I can tell you this. I went to work every day. I held my head high. I come home every day of the week to have a new experience with him. We had to address an issue with him Every day of the week.

Thankfully, I was raised by a father that loved the outdoors. He shared his passion for fishing and hunting. So, the weekends for me were spent in that environment. To be outside in the woods or on the water fishing brought peace to my soul. Nowhere else could I achieve the silence I needed to deal with that marriage or that boy. The two of them became inseparable partners with their lies.

There were times I would take him with me. I tried to show him a side of life that he might learn to enjoy instead of the path he was on, doing for him the same way my father did for me.

This next story will choke me up so prepare yourself."

Lisa: "I have tissues if you need one."

"One hunting season he was old enough to carry his own firearm. I taught him how to shoot and he was fairly good at hitting a target. We ventured out one afternoon to the local game management land. Of course, we did not see any deer and the sun was setting, as the cooler night air was ascending upon us. I did not want to find our way back to the truck in the dark, so we started walking back before it got too dark to see. So, realize we have enough light to see all the way back to the truck. I asked him if he had cleared his gun of any ammunition, including a round in the chamber of the rifle and please double check to confirm the gun was empty. Of course he lied to me, he never checked the rifle or tried to clear any ammunition in the firing chamber.

As we neared the back of the truck I heard his gun fire, the round hit the dirt between my legs. It passed withing a millimeter to my pants. I could feel the bullets wind trail move my jeans as it traveled close to my leg. I am not sure if he tried to hit me or missed by accident that day. I grabbed the gun from him, placing it in the back of the truck.

I could not get mad at him. I should not have trusted him. I did not check the rifle before we started back. I take responsibility for believing he cleared the weapon.

I never told his mother and neither did he."

Lisa: "Did you ever take him hunting again."

"I think you know the answer to your question."

The Evil Within Them

Lisa: "I am ending our session today. That is enough for me. I am sure it is for you also. See you next month."

"Ok, see next month.

After that session with Lisa, I embarked on a long walk through the streets of Columbia, South Carolina. Cool crisp clean air filled my lungs. I needed time to myself. I had retrieved a long-forgotten memory of my past. I summarize the therapy release the trapped information. Lisa had no prior knowledge of the rifle, its report near my leg, Nothing I said previously could have given cause to ask about it. For whatever reason, I just decided to talk about it. I now need to store that memory back where it had been, for thirty years.

The Evil Within Them

58

Session Four

Lisa: "Good afternoon, Michael. How have you been since our last session? You revealed a traumatic experience in our talks. I know patients have difficulty processing memories afterwards. How did you cope with this past month?"

I went for a long walk downtown. A day or two after our session. I reflected on that incident and how close I came to being severely injured or expired from a gunshot wound that day. We were in a remote part of the forest. We had no cell phone at that time and could not call for help. He was too young to provide aid If I need it. Somehow, I recalled that long forgotten memory. You are good at this Doc. How did you get me to remember that?"

Lisa: "I did not have any special power. You did that on your own. Would you like to reflect more about that during today's session?"

The Evil Within Them

"Outdoor experience taught us both a lesson. I had a different outlook on raising him, even continuing to stay married to his mother. Although, I was completely dedicated to making the best of it. The days and years wore me down. He had social problems with school and friends. His Father would pick him up for weekend visits to quickly return him to our door within hours. I am not sure who was to blame for the demise of the visitation schedule. It was a fifty-fifty wild guess, his father's inability to cope with his son or the son's behavior being the defining factor for the return. We never got a straight answer from either."

Lisa: "So, his real father could not accept the son's behavior? I assume if the boy did something wrong it was protocol to return him in leu of any form of disciplinary action to correct his behavior."

"Your assumptions are correct. It was not kosher during those years to administer any type of corporal punishment on a child. He learned quickly from listening to our conversations that he needed his butt whipped once or twice to straighten him out. With his new discovery of his legal rights, he had no problem reporting to us his position of using the protective safety blanket society afforded him. He told us this."

"If you touch me, I will call the police and tell them you assaulted me, and you will go to jail for child abuse."

"Trust me, I was not about to secure a criminal record as a child abuser. I needed my job as a provider and for later in life, it was essential to keep a clean record for the businesses I owned.

We approached every avenue where we could seek answers, to understand his behavior. My wife and I took him to therapists, psychologists, and general practitioners, loathing for information. We attended seminars on attention deficit syndrome. The prescribed drugs he refused to take. We could not convince him or encourage him that medicine was for his own good, that this would change him into an outstanding model person. Absolutely nothing worked. He thwarted every effort we put forth to help him. He would not swallow any pill we gave him, keeping it under his tongue he would spit it out later. We tried putting liquid in his drink only to watch him spit that out. Somehow, he knew what we were trying to give him and sensed the carrier we used to administer the drug with."

Lisa: I am amazed how intelligent this boy was. Did you ever find the clues or in his case the answers you were looking for to help him?"

"No, we found no supportive information from any source we tied. He had a strategically different personality unlike any normal person's behavior. Instead of using his ability for learning or kindness, like a normally developed child, he constantly plotted to upset, destroy, alter, and defy the normality of imagination with his thinking.

As I mention. We attended multiple seminars on subjects related to the problem we had with him. We talked to other parents that were in attendance to share notes with each other. He defied our wildest imagination. Every professional piece of advice we received was met with disastrous results. To sum it up, all anyone could do for us at that point was shrug their shoulders or shake their head in disbelief when we discussed him.

The Evil Within Them

We were, left with no recourse but to accept the be, brought on us and hope he survived in the process."

Lisa: "Give me some examples of his daily activities."

"He was now in middle school, did not ride the bus; we lived in the country and my wife never allowed him to get on one anyway. If he did, he would get kicked off or he would step off the bus anywhere he wanted and never show up to school.

He Should have been on the short bus if you asked me.

So, she dropped him off at school. A couple of hours into his day a teacher would call one of us at work, again no personnel cell phones at the time. The teacher would request we come pick him up and get him out of the classroom. It was always one of the three reasons. He claims he is sick; he is not cooperative or sleeping at his desk. The latter we discovered stemmed from him playing video games all night long. You see when we sent him to his room for the night. He waited until everyone was asleep. He would get up, close his bedroom door, and turn on his game console, turn off the sound and play video games in silence all night, he figured he could sleep in class the next day. But the teachers would not let him, so he told story after story to get out of class.

Lisa: "What did you do about that? Wait, let me guess, your wife took him to the store for a new outfit.?

"For new clothes, Correct answer."

Lisa: "That was a bad pattern to continue with, don't you think."

"Yes, it was. But I could not stand the argument that would ensue if I spoke ill of this procedure. At one point I told him I would take the game set away so he would actually sleep at night like the rest of humanity's normal schedule."

Lisa: "His response to that?"

The Evil Within Them

"He looked at me dead in the eyes and spoke.

"No problem, I know you will give it back to me at some point."

He was clearly satisfied with the temporary removal of the game and functioned simply fine without the game console. He had no problem awaiting the return to him. I was, baffled at his response."

Lisa: "I have no words now. No help from counselors at the school he attended?"

"Like I have mentioned. He continued to defy your wildest intuitions about him. Every piece of normality you would expect to receive from a normal responsive person would be out the window. He would continue to do the very opposite of what you expected. His mind did not function or respond to circumstances or cognitive thinking the same as you or I would."

Lisa: "Did he ever grow out of this? Did he change as he grew older?" You relapsed again, Michael!

The Evil Within Them

"What? Now you are yelling. I was just getting comfortable with the snapping of your fingers."

Lisa: "My apologies. I will snap from now on. Please continue with the thoughts you were contemplating just now in your head."

"He was now at the age we could comfortably and legally leave him at home while my wife and I would go to work or get, invited to a weekend party, or just go out on a date together.

As I mentioned I was an avid lover of the outdoors. I owned a 4-wheeler to ride in the woods on trails while deer hunting or scouting. I kept the key to the machine in a desk drawer in my study at the house. As soon we were gone and out of sight. He would break into the office by picking the lock then find the keys to the 4-wheeler, take it out of the garage and ride it in the dark without lights up and down the road as fast as it would go. One time he crashed it. It sustained severe damage. He somehow managed to get it back in the garage, replacing the key in my study where he found it, re-locked the door, and proceeded to clean himself up so we would not notice his bruises. Honestly, I do not know how he managed to survive the crash.

I discovered the 4-wheeler and the damage days later when I opened the garage door to go ride it myself. It was a total loss. I questioned him about the damage. He stood fast, claiming he had no knowledge to share about the condition of the machine. He kept up his total denial that he had nothing to do with it. He went as far as to tell his Mother I was losing it, that I obviously did not remember crashing the 4-wheeler.

Lisa: "WOW! Let me guess?"

"No, not this time. But I will add this. His mother stood fast with his story. She believed every word that boy manufactured. That was the beginning of her attitude change towards his behavior. Instead of being the interrogator to obtain a truthful statement. She was now in denial he did anything wrong and her aggressiveness towards me of accusing him, performing these events against us was now all my fault somehow."

67

The Evil Within Them

Lisa: "O.M.G. You are telling me she no longer accepted the fact he was at fault and went into denial then began pointing the finger at you as the problem?"

"Absolutely, she was convincing herself I crashed the 4-wheeler and planted it in the garage just to blame her son. As if I was purposefully trying to get him in trouble for no apparent reason."

Lisa: "Did he damage anything else she denied his involvement in?"

"Did he you ask? Yes, he did damage to everything he had contact with.

Months later. I was awarded the contract to do electrical work on a large school project. I bought a brand-new Ford pickup truck. I parked it in our detached garage, awaiting the Union appointed supervisor to get it to start the project. He broke into the study again when the opportunity presented itself and took it for a joy ride. While riding it through mud holes in a pasture, it got stuck in the mud. He then walked to a farm nearby and convinced the farmer to use his tractor to push the truck out of the mud. In doing so, the front bucket of the tractor slipped up off the bumper and crushed the tailgate.

He backed the truck in the garage against the back wall hoping I would not discover the damage. This is how he operated. Damage something, steal something, make it look like he was never involved.

Of course, I discovered the damage days later when I drove it out of the garage when the supervisor arrived. There was on the back tailgate sign of John Deere green paint embedded in the damaged tailgate. Once again there was a heated discussion and denial by both his mother and her son that he did not cause the damage. As we were standing in the driveway arguing over his role in the incident. The next-door neighbor brought her son over to confirm he was with our son when it was, driven out of the garage, driven into a mudhole, then damaged by the farmers' tractor. That ended the investigation. Both the wife and her son stormed into the house with their tails between the legs."

The Evil Within Them

Lisa: "Do I need to guess again what she did?"

"This time you will be correct. New outfit and shoes to match."

Lisa: "Other than the antics of the son you tried to raise. How did you cope with the stress of marriage and dealing with this mischievous stepson? You must have collapsed numerous times under this much duress. Did you ever seek counseling to help you deal with all that? Most people turn to their faith to carry them. Are you religious at all?

"Too many questions to answer at once. I will try to put it in perspective for you. Because someone else has a problem. It is their responsibility in life to address it. I bear no responsibility for the actions of others. Allowing the actions of others to affect your well-being is allowing them to control your emotions and letting them into your mindset and alter the way you prefer to live. Which I prefer to live peacefully. In full control of myself, primarily.

70

The Evil Within Them

I cannot with due respect say, life with them did not affect me from time to time. It Absolutely did. I never broke down in front of anyone. It became necessary to slip away to the peace and quiet of outdoor life. The serenity of sitting under the canopy of a majestic old oak, listening to the sound of the wind, watch a squirrel jump from tree to tree or the song of a bird can transform the most stressful person's lost mind back to himself again quickly."

Lisa: "I agree with you. But I know you are not. Finished. telling me everything I need to hear. Have you?"

"There is more to come, How's the ink holding up in your pen?"

Lisa: "It is shorthand. So, I am good for a while. Please feel free to continue."

"Electrical contracting proved to be challenging. Years you were on top of the world with cashflow

71

and other years not so good. But the bills never changed pace with the cashflow. So, I tendered an offer to buy a restaurant from a man who hired my company to repair the electrical outlets behind his grill. The price was fair, and we closed the deal on January 1, 1994. For years it helped with the difficulties of cashflow and of course paid the bills."

The biggest problem I had was the stepson. When the contracting picked up, I needed to step away from the restaurant to get the project off the ground. When this happened, I let my wife take control of daily activities."

Lisa: "I am sure there is an interesting story I need to hear regarding this."

"Of course, you know there is an interesting story created by the world's best known con artist. Each day the cash register had to balance. Starting cash against the sale of goods. The balancing constantly came short of money. I addressed the situation with the employees to no avail. To get peace of mind and figure out who was stealing. I installed several security cameras. I bet you can guess who my biggest thief was?"

Lisa: "This might be a hard one. So, I will pin the tail on the donkey and speak. The stepson."

"BINGO, correct again."

Lisa: "How many new outfits did he get from the antics at the restaurant provide? Wait, do not answer that rhetorical question. Strike it from the court recordings."

"I think you are enjoying this, aren't you Lisa?"

Lisa: "I am sorry that was out of line. Please continue."

I implemented checks and balances. Bought a new electronic point of sale system where personal codes were needed to open the cash drawer. That

73

worked for a while until Mr. Smarty pants realized he could stand behind the server watching her enter her personal code to open the drawer. She did not catch on to him because he was behind her for only one reason. To watch her enter her code and gain access to the money.

"The next night at closing he cleaned out the cash in the register. Leaving a note that he saw the server do it. He thought the cameras I installed would not see him in the dark. Of course, that old system of cameras could not. But the camera had audio. He could not shut his flapping lips long enough to grab the money and leave. He was bragging to himself while he was stealing the money. His voice was what enabled us to confirm it was him. His lie is now exposed. But as we now know, his mother remained defiant. Even with the evidence she blamed the server and fired her."

Lisa: "You are kidding, right?"

"No, I am dead serious. The cameras continued to reveal a lot of theft from employees as well. One of the cooks I inherited from the purchase of the restaurant was caught om camera in the act of walking out the front door with two cases of beer. As he was walking out with them under arm, he kept an eye on my wife who had her back turned away from him as he quietly left the building, making sure she did not catch him. When I took him to the back room to show him the recording of his dishonest deed. He looked me in the eye and proclaimed the man we were looking at on the monitor was, NOT HIM."

"I had no words for his denial. I just calmly informed him he no longer received a paycheck and please leave.

Lisa: "That is so dishonest. Not only did you deal with a liar and a thief at home. You had to endure more stress from owning the restaurant. How on Earth have you not buckled by this time?"

"Wait, I am about to get to the good part."

Lisa: "Oh NO! I will admit your life is intriguing."

The Evil Within Them

"It will have to be next time. I see by the clock behind you my time has a couple of minutes left. Do you want to bring popcorn for the next session? The plot will be thicker next session."

Lisa: "I will entertain that request. Should I install a soda fountain also?"

"Nice gesture. I will see you next time."

Lisa snaped her fingers but kindly raised her index finger with a gesture for me to remain silent. I rose to my feet and left the room.

The Evil Within Them

No homework for me this time. I left silently and drove out to the country to gather my thoughts. Abuse has many forms. Physical, silent, verbal, or sultry. It can destroy a person slowly within them. The abuser's behavior is a characteristic defined as a mental disorder connected directly to an unstable brain function. Research has now been proven to show that through MRI scanning there is a physical difference in the developmental makeup of the brain within these people.

I have read the research of Sigmund Freud and others seeking clues to the science of behavioral studies. Why did this boy develop the skills to process information he learned then use this information in a criminal or destructive manner? Instead, he chose willfully and systematically to dismantle the very core of normality.

His education came from watching and learning a person's habits, their routine, then figured out how to turn it upside down on them. Instantly!

I have embarked on a personnel journey to understand the process an individual uses in this type of cognitive thinking. A normal brain functions flawlessly in society in work or play, we co-exist with others. To the rest of us know the steps when meeting a new friend or companion for the first time, our brain dissects the spoken word as it subconsciously begins to analyze the content to figure out friend or foe.

This process usually has an immediate response of acceptance, producing the stand or flight scenario. Your decision is based on many factors when you accept friendship or love. It is a natural occurrence of humanity we all unknowingly have. Each person has within their space several close friends we see and interact with daily. We call them or text them. We share our feelings, secrets, and activities. We have trust in them.

Acquaintance type friends are outside of that close circle we protect. They are coworkers, friends of friends, neighbors down the street I use the reference "The Mailman" is that type person. You acknowledge their presence with a fond friendly head nod or a wave of the hand. Occasionally we stand in the grocery store to briefly chat, "how de-does." Then we move on until we bump into them again.

This is a situation where we engage in temporary acceptance of your space that goes no further than that. No explanation why you have decided to leave it at that. You never let them get any closer than a casual encounter. They stay at 'arm's length' and continue to stay in that mode forever. I have no explanation for this type of behavior. It just happens. To you and with them the relationship you have with them never migrates through a casual encounter. You give it no thought to why. This is how our lives become separated from who is in and who is not.

I do believe when you have experienced pain and hurt from a specific period of life, albeit a failed marriage, the loss of a close friend or incidence of betrayal, your personality changes dramatically from close friendship to more of the acquaintance friendships. Subconsciously choosing to feel safer by widening your safe space. You do this by selectively transferring close friends farther away from you as you analyze their true intentions.

Loyal friends you trust will be there forever, they say. I say never trust anyone. There are no true allies.

Everyone has evil within them.

The Evil Within Them

Session Five

Lisa: "I see you have returned to the scene of the crime. I commend you on your dedication to therapy. Most clients have given up on it by the third session."

"No disrespect but, I can see why."

Lisa: "Pardon me"

"That statement reflects my own thinking, rather than an insult to you or your profession."

Lisa: "Got it. So, in our past sessions you have confided with me several times pinpointing the abuse of the person relating to your efforts to raise him.

"Today's session, I would like you to reflect on your marriage and how you and your wife interacted together. Especially about dealing with marital issues and of course raising her son. How did you two get along? What was this like and how do you relate it to your struggles of relationships today?"

The Evil Within Them

"Let me begin saying, when we first met there was a beautiful time where we enjoyed so many activities together. I was into helping my brother-in-law build dirt track race cars. She would go with me to the Saturday night races. We learned to scuba dive together. I bought boats and she went fishing offshore with me.

She did not mind wearing camouflage to sit in a deer stand. We had a wonderful time together. Including intimacy, which we enjoyed nightly with each other before we fell off to sleep.

Lisa: "That is a pretty picture you have painted. Intimacy Nightly? Unusual given the circumstances you have conveyed so far."

"Yes Nightly, unless one of us was sick. We enjoyed each other that much. I mentioned previously we searched for the silver bullet that would make life normal again. We sought peace and tranquility like Ozzy and Harriet family.

The Evil Within Them

That was not to be. As time pressed on, I found the woman I married was changing, showing signs of extreme jealousy of interactions with our friends. She began expressing her unwilling acceptance of me talking to anyone. We began losing friends after friends just because I engaged in conversation during a get together with them. Honestly if it were not from a conversation, the trigger could be anything to set her off. I was always left dumbfounded by the public outburst. So were our friends in attendance.

I recall one instance in Beaufort, South Carolina. We were out to dinner with four other couples. As with every gathering there is always one person in the mix that talks a lot. Captivating the attention of everyone sitting at the table as if he were a guest speaker in a seminar. Going on and on with his story, we all listened intently to his words.

Fuzzy was his nickname. He is sitting at the end of this elongated table in the restaurant rambling about his life. Everyone is looking at him and diligently listening to his story. Suddenly, my wife explodes with expletives directed at me. She begins yelling questions."

"What are you doing looking at her?"

The Evil Within Them

Everyone stops at that moment in disbelief, turning their attention to her. I then calmly ask. "My darling what are you talking about?"

She replies with. "Why are you staring at her?"

"Who?" I ask."

"She points her finger towards fuzzy at the end of her outstretched arm."

"That girl over there behind Fuzzy sitting with that guy against the wall."

"The look of embarrassment on her face when I explained I was not staring at her or anyone other than my friend at the other end of the table. It was just by chance there was a pretty woman with her significant other behind Fuzzy in the same direct line of sight as him. The couple seated there by the wait staff. I was innocently paying attention to his story, nothing else. She jumped to a conclusion based on a line of sight and convinced herself I was more interested in ill intent. We lost four good couples as friends after that."

The Evil Within Them

Lisa: "I honestly do not know how you were able to address that situation as calmly as you indicated."

"We became increasingly isolated from our friends."

"She worked at one of the local banks in town as a teller before I started any of my businesses. I would come in to make a deposit for our checking account from time to time. The other women were very pleasant until I noticed a change in them towards me. I was being treated like I had a disease. No one wanted to be the teller for me or speak to me when I visited.

It was not until the bank Christmas party that one of the women came up to me in confidence with the answer. This person told me my wife was telling the women who she thought was interested in me, that I had cheated on her and gave her something soap and water could not wash off."

Lisa: "WHAT?"

"Yes. Hearing this information was devastating at the time. Her story failed miserably as time progressed, she was unable to adequately answer their inquisitive questioning from her coworkers."

Lisa: "How so, what questions did they ask?"

"The normal questions you would think girlfriends would be asking. What doctor are you seeing? What medications, what was the diagnosis? What are you going to do about this? Are you getting a divorce?"

Lisa: "I see. I would be asking those questions myself. If she could not provide enough clarity, I would assume the coworkers figured out she was a liar."

"Her problem became clear to everyone that she had manufactured these lies about me when the inquisitive questions were, ignored. She could not provide sufficient feedback to support the accusations supporting her claim of my infidelity. She became isolated in

86

her own way. I discovered later while hunting with the husband of a co-worker of hers, my wife fabricated these stories when she overheard some of the ladies discussing their thoughts of what they would do if they were married to me. As I have mentioned previously, I have always been an attractive man. She was afraid to lose me and fail at a second marriage. Her first husband cheated regularly. Once they caught on to her lying. She quit that bank seeking employment elsewhere."

Lisa: "How did you discuss this with her? Explain that please."

"You know that answer before you asked it. It was total denial. She claimed it was someone else who started the rumor and became agitated and defensive. She denied everything and accepted no responsibility for her actions."

"One day I heard it again. She had convinced herself of the lie she was telling people. I made an appointment with a gynecologist to fully examine her. Once he finished with lab tests, he came into the room to announce she was perfectly clean. She had no current sexual transmitted diseases. That shut her up for a good while.

How did I cope with this, you ask?

I could not cope with the argument that would have ensued. I watched my parents argue night after night and day after day. The household turmoil was relentless to live in. There was extraordinarily little peace and quiet. The only peace I had was when my father took me fishing or to the woods to hunt for wild game. I was obsessed with staying after school for every activity I could enroll in, just so I did not have to come home early.

I will provide you with a clear picture of how my parents decided to get married. My Father showed up for a date with my mother one afternoon. All he had was a motorcycle to drive. She met him outside of her house with a bag of clothes, mounted herself behind my dad and said drive, I am never coming back to my drunken physical abusive Father. My parents never drank alcohol while we were still at home.

They got married for convenience and never loved each other."

The Evil Within Them

Lisa: "What a cycle."

"Motorcycle?"

Lisa: "No, The cycle of life. Please, more on the marriage. I want to learn more."

"To understand my wife, I must begin with a little more information on the stepson. You see by the time I bought the restaurant he began to obtain and use drugs more. Of all kinds. He swindled his dealers out of the money for the drugs. They started to show up at the restaurant inquiring into his whereabouts. He was so cunningly talented he would convince them to front him the drugs and that his parents would make good on the payment if he did not return with their money. I did mention he does not think like a normal person, haven't I?"

"When my wife confronted with the demands for money, she would take it out of the cash register drawer. Although this only started after the dealer threatened to do bodily harm to her precious son. Any mother would do the same. These were some scary guys showing up.

He learned a new game and so did the dealers he screwed out of payment. This was now a constant occurrence and his new modus operandi to obtain drugs.

She fell for every fraud he could present to her. She became so complacent about giving out money. Neither she nor him cared who was watching. I saw the son entering the restaurant one afternoon and stepped up next to his mother. She was our cashier and always at the register. Without hearing the discussion, I saw her open the register drawer and hand her son a one-hundred-dollar bill. As he left, I ventured over to inquire into what happened.

Her classic non emotional response came down like a brick on my head. He needs the money for a haircut. Now this boy is a walking talking perfection of a young man manicured to detail unlike anyone I have ever known for his age. He did not need a haircut, nor did he need a hundred dollars for a haircut. He was off to buy drugs. But the ensuing conversation with her was ill fated. She walked away without debating with me.

The Evil Within Them

Her decision to support him monetarily was her decision alone and not up for discussion with me, her husband or anyone inquiring into the transaction.

Even with my declaration that a haircut from the local barber shop I attended weekly was 'SEVEN DOLLARS' not one-hundred-dollars. My voice ignored."

Lisa: "Good gosh, you have been through the ringer. Most men would have already left an abusive relationship of that caliber.

I am sorry I should not provide that type of judgement. Please continue."

"It is quite all right. You are not the only person who tried to slap me in the face to wake me up. The sequence of arguing spilled out into the yard. My neighbor, tired of hearing the noise drove over to our house to pick me up in his truck and go for a drive to de-escalate the situation. I began spouting off and he yelled at me to shut up and chill out."

"Those episodes began a downward spiral of our relationship. My emotional connection with her was now in serious trouble. I began plotting a way out. I needed my sanity to return to normal.

Our next chapter began of decline, strengthened when the son sentenced to a year and six months to the correctional institute. The weekly visits were useless to me. So, I quit attending. Her son would call the house before each scheduled visit and direct his mom to be a carrier of watches and jewelry on her person as she went through security into the facility, then transferred the worn merchandise to her son while in open visitation and in direct sight of guards. They knew what was happening but chose to keep quiet, looking the other way. I could not in good conscience take part in the activity."

"How is the ink holding up in your pen? You are writing increasingly with each session."

Lisa: "I am, the ink is still coming out. I do not believe I have not written this many notes with anyone else. You mentioned the incarceration before but not in such detail. You have also mentioned after his release; he continued a life of crime."

The Evil Within Them

"Yes, he has yet to change his behavior. I often wonder how he has survived all this time without being found on the side of a road or in a dumpster somewhere. But then I remember how cunning he is. I once again tried to give him an alternative outlook on life. My contracting business was doing well so I began playing golf with sales associates and contractor representatives. So, I bought him a set of clubs so he could learn to play with me. He loved the sport and became proficient at the game. We discussed his potential to pursue a career as an instructor and become a professional. It was a better alternative to the activities he was engaged in. This was the caveat I was looking for to turn the corner against his destructive mindset."

"We set a plan of playing on a weekly basis to nurture his game. I began to trust him again and allowed him to charge the round of golf on the club account. Without my supervision he was on his own to practice and gain experience on different courses including my home club course which was equal in difficulty with any PGA sanction course."

"This plan quickly faltered. He crashed golfcart after golfcart into trees or a mudhole while on the course, leaving them where they stopped operating.

93

Rendering them so damaged they had to be replaced by the clubhouse. It took them some time in discovery to pin the damages on his behavior. Again, he claimed innocence of all wrongdoing, even when the attendants wrote down the identifying number of the golf kart he used the day he would play. They were missing carts and began finding damaged carts on the course. The evidence was overwhelming in favor of his rental. In leu of confronting him again, which proved futile. The clubhouse contacted me directly to inform me he was no longer an invited guest and suggest I take a course of action to rectify his behavior."

"They had no idea the mountain I had been climbing for the last 18 years. Again, I will reiterate. Everything I tried, every opportunity I presented to help steer this child, a teenager who was now an adult. Any direction I thought would help give him an upper hand in life was, constantly met with turmoil ending in disastrous conclusions."

Lisa sits silently in her chair. Not leaning on her desk with her arms crossed the way she has done in all our sessions. Her pen is resting on the notepad, she is leaning back in the new office chair in a more comfortable position. I can tell from her facial expression she wants to say something that eludes her now.

I raise my right arm to begin the motion of snapping my fingers to bring her back to me when.

Lisa: "Do not do what you are about to do. That is for me only."

We both smile at each other and share a moment and begin to laugh. She leans forward from the reclining position and once again places her arms on the desk while lacing her fingers together.

Lisa: "Your wife's reaction to all this information was to do what? No, I am not going to mention it was the same response you have conveyed already. Did she always respond with a gift to him for his actions?"

"Always, I never understood her decision to reward the unruly behavior. But yes, she never faltered on that. She was creating a monster."

The Evil Within Them

Lisa: "How so?"

"In my research to find conclusive answers. I began reading scientific studies of behavior in animals. It has been proven you can train an animal to perform a repetitive task if there is a reward once the task is completed. These studies examine human behavior. In one study, participants took turns being the guard in a prison cell scenario.

The study concluded with the craziest results. Each person placed in charge of the others began to morph into a different person using aggressive power over the others once given complete authority. Some were meaner than the others. The rules were clear. No matter what the person in charge ordered them to do, you had to do it, or the study will fail. In conclusion, everyone had a level of evil within them when given the power and control of others.

The old Pavlov's dog theory is another exercise. You give someone the opportunity to have power over another human being, they will continue to extract the golden egg until it is no longer available.

96

The Evil Within Them

In my wife's situation, her son owned the power over her to extract anything he wanted or available to him, including money, "lots of money." There was no limit to the extravagant schemes of extortion he produced. She had been conditioned to provide without question of why or what for, and without reasoning."

Lisa: "Interesting analysis. Because you concluded she was under her son's control, is this your reasoning for staying with her in marriage?"

"True. Other reasons were prominent, like the sanctity of marriage. I did not wish to start over, we had a daughter, I am no quitter, things like that. But I will say, she became increasingly influenced by his requests. I can honestly say, I tried in vain to understand the connection. Other people saw his control over her. Repeatedly employees confided in me. Asking what is going on with them?"

Lisa: "Daughter, you have not mentioned her."

97

The Evil Within Them

"She is my heart, my reason for living. I had firsthand understood what a broken marriage can do to a child, and I was determined through all the hell I went through. I was not going to let this scenario happen to her. She was going to have her father and Mother together until she was old enough to understand the truth."

Lisa: "Commendable behavior, you sir deserves a medal for your determination. Our time once again ends, and this pen is out of ink."

"See you next month Michael."

"I will see my way out. Until next time. By the way I know you want to know how I interacted with my wife. I need you to understand the son's manipulation to understand how we fell apart in the end and how we became increasingly distant with each other."

"Make a note to ask me about the drinking when I return."

The Evil Within Them

I once again walk out of Lisa's office to breath in the cool crisp air of Autum. It is refreshing to fill my lungs and begin my solitary walk to clear my head.

Talking to Lisa is healing my soul, but remembering the details of a life I hated consumes me.

The Evil Within Them

Session Six

Once again, I walk into Lisa's office, exchange the usual pleasantries, and sit in the new comfortable chair. Something is different with the room. I have always had a photogenic memory. I notice minute changes to the environment around me. I begin by looking at Lisa, our eye contact is a dead giveaway, she has a slight smirk on her face. The way a person looks at you during a poker game. I am reading her expression. My situational awareness is in high gear; I pan the room with my eyes. Assessing the framed pictures of family and dogs on the wall, her credentials were framed and notarized from her Ivy League University. An eight by eleven paper documentation authorizing her to provide therapy. Nothing obvious there. The chair I am using, and the chase lounge she replaced a few months prior remain the same. I look back at the top of the desk, I see the old coffee cup holding an array of pens and pencils, it still says "Best Therapist ever." Along the side of that cup is a stack of multicolored files, each with a name tag of clients. I assume retrieved from a file cabinet for the daily procession of patients visiting. No Hard-wired phone anymore. Everyone uses a cell phone. Lisa's desk is always neat, uncluttered, and clean.

101

The Evil Within Them

"What is that?" I ask, pointing out a small white instrument placed on the desk near her, the size of an individual cigarette box with small air holes dotting its surface.

I looked up at Lisa, established eye contact again, awaiting her reply. She has a faint grin forming. That, I gotcha grin.

Lisa: "I have decided to step away from the pen and pencil method of keeping records while my clients are talking. Sometimes I miss part of the conversations when I am concentrating on writing notes, this system provides a more efficient process."

"I have installed a Bluetooth recording device with a subscribed service to automatically transcribe our conversations. I can then review every spoken word sent to my computer screen later and before the client comes back for the next session. It helps me remember what we talked about. This modern technology prevents me from missing valuable information."

"Legally I am supposed to inform my clients before turning it on. You do not need to sign a waiver of writes or anything. So, if you are comfortable with the recorder? Do I have your permission?"

I squirm in the chair as I respond. I was comfortable watching you diligently keep up with your pen. So, if this enables you to increase your efficiency, giving you more time to engage with clients like me, then I am happy to allow you to record our conversations.

I watched Lisa turn away from our eye contact to look at the device. She begins to stroke the top of the new device with the palm of her hand as if she had a new cat to play with. I could tell this new machine made her happy. Her grin turned into a huge smile.

Lisa: "Thank you. I will start recording now. You mentioned as you left last month, I should remind you of the drinking. Did your wife start drinking? Continue drinking? I assume she overindulged a somewhat?"

"Yes, lots of alcohol. When we traded the beach house to the buyer of my restaurant we left Fripp Island, South Carolina. It was an even monetary trade. Once back up in operation we needed to hire staff to help us run it. We chose a middle-aged woman with wait staff experience. Her husband dropped her off to the restaurant on his way to another job that kept him on duty past her daily punch out time. She used to wait for him to come to get her later that evening. One day she asked my wife for a ride home. This ride home turned into a stop for cocktails, thus the beginning of the late-night binge drinking session.

"I discussed the issue with my wife to no avail. She saw no problem with her actions. So, I fired the server with the idea my wife would stop drinking and start coming home at a decent hour. To my surprise she went out drinking on her own. Night after night I would close the restaurant and head home to an empty house. I would then venture bock into town to find her car parked outside of a bar, walk inside and retrieve her then follow her vehicle as she drove home."

Lisa: How often did this scenario play out? Did this become a big problem for you?"

"This was an everyday occurrence which escalated into a huge problem. Especially when she began hiding her car behind the bars in the alley or down the street out of sight. This increased the difficulty of finding her, I could not readily find what watering hole she was in. I then adapted my search tactics to walking bar to bar until I found the bar seat she was occupying. First, she would agree to come home with me. When she became so addicted to drinking the situation escalated to a higher level.

Lisa: "Escalated? How so?"

"She became so intoxicated with her drinking; she was unable to sign her name to the credit card receipt. I began paying the tabs, but the gravity of the situation did not end there. She became belligerent when asked to stop drinking and come home with me. It was now obvious that she could not drive herself in her own car. I had to lift her off the bar stool, she was extremely intoxicated and could not walk at all. There was nothing I could do but carry her to my vehicle."

"When we arrived home, I carried her to the sofa or the bed. Fully clothed, she slept that way until the sun rose the next day, then prepared herself for a return to work.

Lisa: "You were taking care of her like you would a child or her son."

"I was, but she acted like a child. Here is the issue I dealt with. Because I was recovering from a different bar nightly; her car had to be left downtown. This means I woke up every day to drive into the restaurant for startup with the other employees. Then before our lunch crowd arrived, I had to drive home to get her, then drive back to collaborate with her so she could then use her car."

"This became the nightmare of all nightmares as she repeated this process day after day. I was getting tired of it. I pleaded with her to stop. I pointed out the dangers of drinking and driving. She could hurt or kill an innocent person. The possibility of losing our business to a lawsuit never deterred her relentless pursuit of alcohol.

"She was on a destructive path. I finally had enough and stopped coming back to get her for work. I

106

had to fire my own wife to slow her down. All I accomplished was slow down her drinking. Eventually she quit the practice of late-night bar hoping and stayed home to drink. I figured she must have had a premonition or something. All the begging and pleading I did to get her to see the evil in what she was doing to herself, and our family got her thinking."

"At least I was able to breathe a little bit. The dangers of her driving while highly intoxicated had stopped. The heavy drinking never did. I lost my wife, the woman I loved, the mother of my only child."

"My wife loved a bottle of alcohol more than she loved me. Night after night I would come home from the restaurant, sit down and watch tv by myself. She was aways there after that. When I say she was there I mean she was home, although three sheets into the wind, a bottle deep or a twelve-pack consumed. At the end of the night, I would try to wake her for bed. That worked a few times then I quit trying and left her on the sofa with a beer bottle spilled on her chest and our boxer dogs licking the slobber off her face."

"She was a beautiful woman with blonde hair, with the type of female figure all women were envious of. She could have been Victoria's Secret model if she

107

wanted it. I nicknamed her Blondie. She ruined my feelings for her with the drinking. Her son would egg it on with his drunken demeanor, then the alcohol induced arguments began. The arguments became intense when her son would tell a fictitious lie about me."

Lisa: "I know this pattern well, I see many clients with the same issue. I am sure the son trying to intimidate his mom to intentionally ruin your marriage took a toll on you."

"You are correct. I discussed this very issue with her to no avail. He would start drinking alongside her at home, then begin his mind game of manipulation. Telling her I was cheating on her, or he figured I was not running the restaurant properly. The story was always fabricated to intimidate his mom. His mind game worked so well; I came home to a two-person mob every night. The drinking affected her memory of the arguments so much the next morning she had no recollection of the night before and acted like nothing had ever been, said to me. She lost all recall of the event."

The Evil Within Them

"I struggled with my reasoning to stay and work it out or leave forever. At that point in our marriage, I wanted this living nightmare to end so badly, I set the wheels in motion to end the marriage. It was a decision I became increasingly comfortable with making. There was no alternative. I struggled with my sanity. I was losing the battle to stay in the marriage and it no longer made sense to continue."

"It was me or him who needed to leave and I mean in a way he would never return. The thought of jail time for a heinous act was not in me or of my character."

"One day a customer and his wife became regulars at happy hour. We became friends. He saw firsthand the crazy things my stepson was capable of. He became a confidante; I turned to him often to express my desire to end my marriage. I informed him of how many times I had previously left the household, only to return with promises that were, never kept for long."

The Evil Within Them

Lisa: "Tell me a little more about your friend. Let us change for a moment. You need a momentary change in your thoughts. What was his name?"

"Honestly, I cannot recall his name or his wife's name. It has been too many years, albeit, I do know they have passed away. They were the nicest couple. A daily rendezvous at three o'clock or shortly thereafter. You could almost set your watch to their arrival through the door to their pair of bar stools. They decided it was the perfect spot at the bar. He was an insurance fraud investigator and knew a lot of people from all over the country."

"As I mentioned he became my confidante, asking several questions about my background in electrical work and other ability besides the restaurant. It was a few weeks after I revealed I was an electrical contractor, he asked if I was interested in applying for an electrical project manager's position with a large company in Las Vegas, Nevada. He mentions this move would be my ticket to finally get my divorce and sanity returned."

"This was the opportunity for which I was waiting. I wrote a resume. My friend reviewed it and

110

recommended I adjust the format. Once completed he sent it off to his friend in Vegas. Two weeks later I was sitting in Mohave Electric's office interviewing. Later that night I accepted an offer to come to Las Vegas."

Lisa: "How did she take the news you were off to Las Vegas?"

"At first, she and her son were, elated to be rid of me and my constant request of them to clean up their actions. They were now free to do whatever they wished, whenever they wanted without me in the picture to insist on keeping decency and controls."

Lisa: "I will bet a dollar that did not go well for them. I am, assured things got out of control quickly without you being around."

"You are bating a thousand Lisa. She did not last six months in her attempt to run the restaurant by herself with that son of hers running it on the ground. She was not much better off herself, quickly losing control of it.

111

The Evil Within Them

The alcohol flowed freely, and I mean to all the customers. She began buying drinks for everyone daily at happy hour. She began buying the customers' loyalty. They were laughing so badly behind her back. The customers she thought were her friends continued taking advantage of the situation, after all it was free beer and cocktails. Who would turn that down?"

"A little more to add before I end this story about her efforts to keep the restaurant running. Her son would constantly walk into the restaurant at night after his mom would leave. Walk over to the register, punch the no sale button to open the drawer. He would then take hundreds of dollars out to fund his own drug deals or partying around town."

"My wife would always blame the night server for taking the money. It did not matter to her when they tried to tell her it was her sone and not them. She defied all reasoning by ignoring the information presented. This started the proverbial snowball rolling downhill. The wait staff began stealing money for themselves."

Lisa: "You need to author a book about all this someday. I am sure it will be a bestseller."

The Evil Within Them

"I just might someday. I need to tell you one more thing about her son and my wife before I leave today while it is fresh in my mind."

Lisa: "We may go over in time, but I have no more clients scheduled today, please go ahead."

"She was so defiant about his behavior. It was winter and we decided to go to Beach Mountain, North Carolina to snow ski for one year. He was about fifteen or sixteen years old. I upfitted everyone with the equipment necessary to endure the wintry weather."

"One evening we could not stop him from going back to the slopes to ski at night. We tried diligently to tell him he needed aa additional lift ticket to allow night skiing, and we were not going to pay for it. He would not believe us. So, we let him find out for himself without any money to purchase a ticket. About an hour and a half later, we got a call from the mountain police. He was in custody for trespassing without a night lift ticket to ski."

113

The Evil Within Them

"The encounter with him was so intense, the officers involved had to pull draw their service revolvers on him to stop him from getting on one of the lifts to the top of the mountain. He was so adamantly defiant to get on the lift that he was, almost shot in apprehending him."

"It has been, mentioned to me on several occasions, I need to author a book about my life with him and her too many times already. My time is up for today. No need to say good-bye I am out of here."

Lisa: "I am getting a clear picture of this evil person you tried to raise together. Go for your walk now, I will see you next time."

Session Seven

Lisa: "Good morning, Michael. I have been reviewing the transcripts of our earlier sessions. I found where you interviewed for a project manager's position in Las Vegas, Nevada, Is that correct? Tell me a little more about your time out there. Specifically, what was your job, and did you have any relationships while you were there? I know when people break up or get divorced, they always try to find a replacement for what they lost or needed they did not get from the past relationship. Many times, this does not work out.

I see Lisa beginning the motion of lifting her hand to snap those fingers to bring me back to reality.

"HOLD UP! I shout. I am recalling memories that have been locked away for years so, give me a second before you snap away at me. I did have a few relationships. Most of them never worked out for any given period. It was suggested that I try a dating site. Figuring this should be easy to find a nice person without a darling of a son like the one I distanced myself from with the divorce. My wife divorced me as soon as I left the house. I gave her everything we owned, including the restaurant I owned, the house we shared. I was desperate to be free of her son's antics, I gave up everything for the peace and quiet I deserved."

Lisa: "I see this a lot."

"Let me begin with the online dating site of that period. The tv commercials for E-Harmony were on every channel. With that in mind I signed up for a three-month period.

Lisa: "That sound like a clever idea. How did that work for you? Did you meet anyone?"

"Funny you should ask. It did not take me long to realize the mistake of trying an online service was not for me. After two weeks of viewing profiles of women, I decided to try one lady whose profile picture caught my attention, she looked extremely attractive, close to my age. This was working seamlessly. We had the same interest in golf and other aspects of life."

The Evil Within Them

"We chatted through the site and finally exchanged phone numbers, agreeing to meet in person at a local golf course to have a round of golf. Completing a four-hour round of golf should provide an understanding of each other if it was going to work between us. We would move forward from there or shake hands and part ways. I arrived at the course on schedule. Grabbed my clubs from the trunk of the car and went ahead to the clubhouse. There was a woman already on the practice putting green. I set my clubs down next to the green and walked into the clubhouse looking for my date. No one was in the club house except the male attendant. I began enquiring if he had seen the lady in question, I was to play a round with. He calmly said: "She is here on the practice green now.""

"Lisa, I will tell you this experience was my first at realizing women post pictures of themselves from high school for their profiles. Not a recent one. I walked right passed this woman within a couple of feet of her. What a transformation forty years does to some people. She looked terrible in comparison to her profile picture. I felt so betrayed. Out of respect I did finish our round of golf but never spoke to her again. The potential relationship started off on the wrong footing."

117

The Evil Within Them

Lisa: "What did you do? How did you recover from that encounter?"

"I at once cancelled my subscription to the dating site. Of course, they asked me to reply why I requested the cancellation prior to the three-month term."

This was my email response.

In consideration of the process of finding a match for myself. I found the service you provide is less than adequate. The fees paid do not include checking details or photo matching of the individuals using the service. I highly recommend you consider a corporate name change from E-Harmony.com to E-Homely.com.

"I received my cancellation without a response from them."

Lisa: "O.M.G.! You did not actually send that message, did you?"

"I absolutely did. Word for word."

The Evil Within Them

Lisa: "I cannot believe you sent that message. Although I do understand your position. Especially with first-hand experience with someone who obviously was purposefully deceiving you by posting false information. It is a devious evil way to attract a person to your profile."

"It is not just women who do this. I know of men desperate enough to post old masculine pictures of themselves also."

Lisa: "I have no doubt this happens on every match making site there is. Was there anyone else that you had an interest in while you were out there?"

"Yes, there was. Toni, she was a special person. Very kindhearted woman. The first lady I ever dated was older than me by ten years. I frequented a small one-off Italian restaurant where she worked the night shift as a server. She approached me one day as I was playing the one-armed bandits."

119

The Evil Within Them

Lisa: "A what?"

"That is the nickname people gave slot machines that had one handle to pull down to start the machines' function. So, Toni served me drinks and began striking up conversations every time she returned. Soon I knew a lot about her from hearing her talk when she would return with my cocktail. Oh' Boy could Toni talk."

"One thing led to another, and we soon moved in together. Of course it was a strange relationship. I worked days as an electrical project manager, and she was a night shift server. We hardly saw each other during the week. But the weekends were full of fun and Toni never shut up. She had two female roommates until I moved in with her. Then she ran them off quickly. Typical territorial jealousy took precedence over the extra income for the mortgage."

"We shared a lot in common except the talking. It was 2008 when the housing bubble dried up a lot of project funding. Including Aria at the Las Vegas City Center. I was the electrical project manager for the building. One day the owners I worked for met in my office when I arrived at my office. It was severance time. The project had funding pulled by Deutch Bank. That project and every project funded by a bank now shuttered all over town."

"The company I worked for provided a large severance package, and I went out the door. Not fully understanding the gravity of the collapse of our economy I tried to find another job as quickly as possible. This proved to be a lesson of great proportions. No one was able to hire anyone. So, for the first time in my life, I felt unemployment. I then packed my bags, loaded them into my car and drove back to South Carolina."

Lisa: "I am getting information that Toni was not mean or obnoxious in any way to you, am I hearing you correctly? Why Did you leave Vegas and her?"

"There were no jobs anywhere that paid the money I made. I worked the math. It made more sense to file for unemployment than work with my hands and tools at a lower paying position.

121

The Evil Within Them

Toni was a darling, but I needed a job. And I found it back in South Carolina. I loved her but was not "in" Love with her."

Lisa: "This is getting interesting. Let me get my popcorn."

"You have popcorn?"

Lisa: "No silly, I'm using a metaphor."

"Oh! Ok then."

Lisa: "Tell me what happened when you came back from Las Vegas."

"It was a crazy time. I had to move in with a friend because of the divorce settlement, I had signed over the ownership of the restaurant and my house to my wife. Now my ex-wife." Once she found out I had

returned she contacted me about buying back the restaurant I had given up in the divorce.

Lisa: "Did you buy it back?"

"Yes, I did. At a premium of what it was worth
at the time."

Lisa: "If you want something bad enough you
will do anything to acquire it. Please share those details
you can."

"I met with her a few times to discuss the price
I would have to pay to buy back a restaurant I purchased
with my money and gave away." you better get popcorn
Lisa or sit back in your seat this is explosive. I agreed
to buy back my restaurant for half a million dollars, paid
to her out in weekly amounts over eight years."

Lisa: "Holy Cow!"

The Evil Within Them

"That is not the bad part. Hold on tight missy. This bronco is not tamed yet. I made several attempts to help guide her to invest this money and to get a job so she could put this money away for retirement time. Of course, she refused to listen and spent the twelve-hundred-dollar payments I made to her account every week sitting at a bar drinking it away. The weekly Friday installments were frequently followed with a request for advancement on Monday of the next week. I refused every time."

Lisa: "How did she spend that much money every week?"

"I have no clue how she did it. But she did. I am convinced a lot of it swindled out of her account by her son. He was so good at it. He would call his mom and ask for her debit card numbers, claiming he was at a filling station out of gas, with no money to buy gas. She would convey her debit card number, end date and CVC code over the phone, believing she was helping her poor son. He would memorize the numbers and go on a shopping spree or to an ATM to get money for drugs. He

124

knew exactly what money she was getting from me and when it would hit her bank account. She was so dumb, she allowed this scheme of his to continue for years, she constantly called the bank or me to verify I made her deposit. She refused to accept this evil-minded son could do such a thing to her."

"Once the payments stopped and money dried up, she was, now broke. She once again needed money and offered me a deal to buy the house I gave her in the divorce. Once again, we confirmed a price of twenty-five-thousand dollars for the equity in the house and she signed it over to me. I then had my house and my restaurant back in my possession. There is only one problem to deal with when I had the keys in hand. I went to the house to start moving in. Unknown to me, the interior walls, including every interior door, were destroyed. Large holes punched into the walls and wooden doors from the rage of her son."

Lisa: "She did not think it important to inform you of the damage first? Let me guess, she spent all that money too?"

The Evil Within Them

"One hundred percent correct. Here is the warning."

Lisa: "What now? There is more to this story?"

"After that money dried up, she called me to ask for a job."

Lisa: "Say it isn't so."

"It is so. I desperately needed a dependable employee, so, I gave in and hired her as a cashier. To this day she works for twelve dollars an hour for my daughter. I still have a tough time understanding the mentality of how she was manipulated by her son. He skillfully pried that money away from her without her suspecting any of the schemes he used on her. She loved his evil ways, unconditionally."

Lisa: "Has the stepson ever had a job or kept one for any length of time? I realize you tried to help while you were at home, but beyond that period did he ever succeed at anything?"

"He is now forty-six years old. He has had multiple opportunities and positions. He has failed to keep even one job for any length of time. The story told is the same repeatedly, the company he works for is not a well-oiled machine, or the employees ganged up on him, they do not know how to run a business. All his excuses and reasoning for losing a job fall into the same category of blaming the company.

"His Mother still has not caught on to his lies."

"I concluded a mother's love for her child and his excuses reaches far beyond the reality of normal human behavior. She was a direct witness to him stealing a car and followed by the police and immediately returning to the scene with him in handcuffs for her to identify him as the perpetrator. She herself saw him steal the car. She would look the arresting officer in the eye, proclaiming they had the wrong person, that he did not steal the car. Then she would attack the arresting officer's character for wrongfully chasing and arresting her innocent son."

127

The Evil Within Them

Lisa: "They were in this together, weren't they?"

"Like two peas in a pod, partners in crime I used to say. I have another incident to share today that comes to me, if you are interested in hearing another evil episode?

Lisa: "Lay it on me. I need more popcorn. Please go ahead, Michael. Get it out, you really need to express yourself. This is the process I described in our first meeting. I am here to listen to what you have locked away. So, let us begin unlocking all those thoughts."

"It was 1995. My contracting business was in its prime. The renovations at the restaurant I bought were complete and sales exceeded all expectations to the point I needed to personally work in the restaurant daily to keep up with the number of customers coming in for lunch. The call-in phone orders were so overwhelming we would take the phone off the hook, so we did not have to listen to it constantly ringing. One of the employees saw the phone receiver lying beside the phone base and decided to place it back on top of the holder. This started the ringing again."

"I was a little uneasy about that as I walked over to answer the phone. It was my stepson. Now he had not been back home for quite some time. These absences never triggered any concern, it was now a common occurrence with him so, we knew he was with friends doing stupid things or at a crack house doing drugs. Honestly, I figured one day the state troopers would show up with the sad news."

Lisa: "What did he want when he called?"

"He wanted into the house, he demanded to get into the house. We never let him have a key to the front door because of his behavior we assumed he would come home one day and clean us out. Well, on that day he called asking me to leave my busy restaurant full of customers to come and let him into the house. I simply

129

replied I could not leave now, but I would be home in a couple of hours when the crowd thinned out."

"My answer was, met with filthy language declaring he would find a way in. I tried to still be calm as the conversation escalated to wild threats of killing me if I and when I came home. This was now his standards of operation; to use threatening language to intimidate his mom and this day he was trying this new tactic on me."

"Of course, this declaration from him was now at a level I needed to involve the sherif. Now enroute to the house with the sherif officers in tow. We arrived at the house. To my surprise he had torn down our beautiful stained French entry doors to our house to gain entry. To no one is surprised he was high on crack cocaine the entire day. His mind was not thinking rationally."

"The officers attending asked if I wished to press charges or just remove him from the premises, since he was a resident there was not a lot of legal footing in this situation. Their hands tied by the law."

"I had no choice but to accept the damage. Then they took him from the property. Where they dropped him off is a mystery. More than likely, it was another crack house. We did not see him for a week after that."

"I then drove to Home Depot to purchase new entry doors and spending half the night tearing out the damaged ones and replacing them with the new doors I purchased."

I sat in silence for some time remembering the pain filling my soul again with the hate and disgust for him I endured that day. Lisa refrained from snaping her fingers. This time she left me alone as I wiped tears from my cheeks.

That day changed me forever.

Lisa: "I see this story is extremely emotional for you. Having to repair the damage he caused to your home, threatened with your life at the same time, having a strong will to support yourself to not escalate the threat he made to you. You did the right thing Michael. Getting public safety there to defuse the situation was the right choice. You do realize the choice you made that day has saved your life?"

131

The Evil Within Them

"Yes, I understand that. It is extremely difficult to talk about it even today, after all these years."

Lisa: "What did your wife think of all this?"

"She saw the damage he did. She knew he was on drugs at the time. This was not his normal level of evil behavior. The drugs played a significant role in escalating his behavior, she helped me replace the doors, never saying a word while we were working."

Lisa: "I hope she didn't go buy him a new outfit."

"No, not this time. I could not tell her the whole story. I know she would not believe me. There were too many times he had broken into the house through windows before. She never accepted the proof he had broken windows to enter the house when we were away. She constantly refused to accept his evil behavior. I saw no point in discussing his elevated threat to me. She would never accept it as the truth. I am assuring you she

132

would have turned the tide and blamed me or blatantly call me out as a liar."

Lisa: "Why would she do that to you?"

"It is the Motherly bond to her son. He would convince her he had no role in the incident, or I was lying to her about him to get him in trouble. That is how his mind operated. He was so convincing she believed no information anyone brought to her attention regarding his antics."

Lisa: "Our time is up today. I know you need a break and so do I after this session. Have a great ay Michael. See you next month.

No words exchanged beyond that goodbye; I left Lisa's office for another solitary walk.

The Evil Within Them

Session Eight

I have begun walking to Lisa's office. The streets a bustling with vehicles at every intersection I come to. People walking without speaking, I remember a song by Simon and Garfunkel.

'The sound of silence'

Although the original artist is not singing, the version I hear playing is performed by a different generation. The rendition by "Disturbed" is now playing in my head. This man's voice is overwhelmingly powerful singing his version.

I notice everyone I pass on the sidewalk is entranced in their own thoughts. No one engages in a stranger these days. If I were to strike up a conversation with a total stranger, it would not go well. The facial expression received would frighten Frankenstein himself.

I stand taller than most people, enabling me to see over them and ahead of me, no danger lurking just a sea of people walking to a destination. I stop at the intersection a few blocks from the building housing Lisa's office, taking a moment to see my surroundings. Humanity is complex, genetics play a significant role in who we are and what we become. No one chooses your DNA.

As I take this moment in time, I see variations of human coding that forms us into our shape, tall, thin, short, round, redheads, blonde, graying with age.

How we walk and speak are identifiably different in a way that gives our character identity. We can tell who is speaking to us from the voice we hear. The signature walk of a person is another identifier. The friend or foe, flight or fight ingrained in all of us.

I find myself standing next to this brick building watching the movement of people, cars and a few pigeons flying overhead, we are all in constant motion until our final days.

I need to start moving, Lisa is waiting for me to arrive.

Lisa: "Good morning, Michael, Good to see you again. How are you doing? What have you been up to since our last session?

The Evil Within Them

Lisa has a big smile on her face. She is a happy person today. I question why.

"Lisa, what have you been smoking? You have a vibrant personality today. It is Monday, which is usually gloomy for most people returning from a weekend to their office or laboring job. What is on your mind little lady. Did you get some this past weekend?"

For reasons beyond my comprehension, I felt compelled to ask that silly question. I feel like her therapist now.

Lisa: "I might have but that is none of your business."

"Please excuse me Lisa, I am breaking the ice here. Is there something you need to talk about with me today? It is ok if we reverse rolls."

Lisa: "No not today. I am the therapist you are a client. Let us leave it at that. Now, what would you like to discuss today? This is your session. I have the recorder charged up and ready to start it. I reviewed the transcript of our last session. I like this modern technology."

"I get it now; you are smiling because you've turned into a techno geek."

Lisa: "I admire your observation of me, but can we get on track. You have an hour to use, and fifteen minutes are already gone."

"Ok, back to my time in Vegas. I mention using E-Harmony or as I referred to the site as E-Homely. That was a mistake. I stumbled upon Match.com, this site proved to be itself to be no better than E-Homely. I met a lady who misrepresented herself the same thing as the last one. She had some desperation to find a mate. Her profile picture looked pleasing enough to try her. Again, the meeting turned South quickly when I realized she liked a dozen doughnuts more than she liked herself. I will not go into more details; you get the mental picture."

"Off I go again searching the internet when the algorithm in the Yahoo browser indicated I should try a more sophisticated dating site."

138

The Evil Within Them

Lisa: "You are pausing, what was the name of this site?"

"You must promise not to laugh or scold me when I reveal it. Please reserve judgement until I explain the details."

Lisa: "Do we need to lock fingers and pinky swear to never reveal the information I am about to receive?"

"Not necessary."

Lisa: "You are blushing. What is the name of the site you chose to use?"

Lisa triggers me as I blurt out the name of the site.

"SUGARDADDY.COM"

"There I said it."

The Evil Within Them

Lisa is cracking up with uncontrollable laughing. All I could do was smile and laugh with her.

"Hey, all I can say is it worked for me. The site has a weird connotation of a name. But it is a higher end dating site for elite individuals that do not want wish to be bothered with the inaccurate details of the other site. Everyone signed up is, scrutinized and verified as a real person." Laugh away Lisa, I get it."

"Would you be interested in getting out of here? Let us get a pizza."

Lisa: "I do not think that would be proper to go out with you. I would like to keep our sessions on a professional level."

"Do not flatter yourself Lisa. I am suggesting we get out of this box we are in and continue this session while eating lunch, I am hungry for a pizza. You receive the same money sitting here or out enjoying a pizza. What do you say to that?"

The Evil Within Them

Lisa: "Pizza sounds good."

We both stand up to leave the four-square walls of Lisa's office. I was feeling cramped up being in there. I needed a different environment to talk to her. Lisa rose from her seat as we walked out of her office to the streets of downtown Columbia, South Carolina. I am always aware of my surroundings, especially aware of the people I am in direct contact with.

Our destination was not far away, as we began our walk to the pizza place, I became aware of Lisa's height in comparison to mine. I am six foot one, Lisa is four foot eleven. A simple error in my judgement, she was always sitting in her chair when I arrived for my sessions with her.

Arriving at the pizza place we were seated at a table with a window view of a side street, which is good for me because movement gave me cause to investigate.

Lisa: "Michael, we have ordered the pizza, and you can now relax. Tell me more about Las Vegas. You mentioned the website you chose to use for matching up with a potential mate."

141

The Evil Within Them

"I know that site sounds more like a hookup site, but I can assure you it was quite different than you would expect. I was cautious at first, then realized there were upper class profiles that caught my attention. I eventually met a classy lady. At least initially she presented herself like she was."

Lisa: "Another fake photo posted of herself to get your attention?"

"Not this time. I selected a nice restaurant for our first meeting. Trust me, I was relieved that she looked exactly like her profile photo. We hit it off well enough and agreed to continue seeing each other."

Lisa: "This sounds like you found a good woman to be with, how did it end?"

"You know me by now, don't you? I will begin with this. In the beginning of searching for a companion

The Evil Within Them

I was very trusting. I did my best to make every relationship work out.

Her story went like this; she was the widow of a
prominent international bank president who adored her
and provided well for her. When her uncle fell ill with
cancer, she moved into his house to care for him in his
final days on earth. She claimed to be a registered nurse,
which is how she met her husband when he visited the
doctor's office she worked at, nothing strange with all
that and I thought nothing of it.

Lisa: "Something triggered you about the relationship you did not accept." Am I correct?"

"That question is why I keep coming to see you.
It is your sixth sense. You know things are not kosher."

"I did the manly thing of working during the
day. I would contact her afterwards to pick her up for
an evening together. Eventually she accepted nightly
residence at my apartment. Then I took her home the
next day to care for her uncle. Now, understand I was
ok with the routine until I became frustrated waiting for

her to prepare herself for the return trip. He decided I needed morning inspiration before we got out of bed.

Lisa: "Oh boy, I need to order a beer and have a cigarette with my slice of pizza. Please continue with any details of your morning you want to share with me currently."

"Later, not here Lisa! Eat your pizza."

"Here is the warning I had to deal with. The routine of picking her up and dropping her off the next morning drained my emotions. Driving around I215 in Las Vegas in morning rush hour traffic became a nightmare I could no longer tolerate. So, one day I asked her if she could drive herself over to my apartment instead of me being her daily chauffeur.

Loisa: "How did that work out for the relationship between you two?"

144

The Evil Within Them

"Lisa, she informed me she had no vehicle to drive, furthermore she did not have a driver's license to drive in Las Vegas. This was my first encounter with a professional manipulator. She really did not want or needed a relationship, she needed an out, away from her dying uncle and whatever she needed to do to achieve her goal, she performed the necessary tasks to conduct it. Including sleeping with me."

I look at Lisa, she has a mouthful of pizza, stopped chewing, and swallowed it whole. Wiped the red sauce from her fingers with a fresh napkin and responded.

Lisa: "Are you sure she wasn't a call girl in disguise?"

"Very plausible, I do not know. I do know I began backing off with the weekday visitation and reduced seeing her to the weekends only. I merely pointed out the trouble it was to travel the distance every morning to drop her off and I was late for work too often. I did not want to lose my job over her. She agreed and that was the end of the weekday overnighters. She felt bad about the driver's license situation and not having transportation. So, she bought a Harley Davidson motorcycle."

Lisa: "She bought a motorcycle?"

"Indeed, she did. The rest of this story is comical. She had no idea how to ride the thing, never owned or drove one at fifty years old."

Lisa: "What was she thinking?"

"She always wanted one, she loved the way bikers dressed up to ride. She bought the Harley and enrolled in training from the dealership. In Nevada you had to have certified operators training to get a motorcycle license. She enrolled and eventually passed the test. Of course, she had several setbacks but eventually got certified. The school sent her on her way with a certification she should have never received."

Lisa: "Stop eating for a second, I want to hear this. Obviously, something happened to her."

146

The Evil Within Them

"Wow you have a sixth sense of what is coming don't you?"

Wel, about a week later she had joined a group of other riders for a Sunday ride out to the desert. She cranked up the machine, put it in gear, headed out to the intersection near her uncle's house, lost control of the motorcycle and crashed through the neighbor's fence into the side of their house. Broke her leg in hitting the house."

Lisa: "Oh lord that poor girl."

"Oh no do not feel sorry for her. You see, while she was in the training sessions she became friendly with another biker getting his certification.

Lisa: "Don't tell me she was cheating on you?"

"Just my luck, she was sleeping with him during the week and me on the weekends. The good part of this story is I really did not care for her, I knew she was using me anyway. I accepted the news gracefully. It was an effortless way out of that relationship for me."

Lisa: "I understand the discomfort most people feel when they receive the news or discover a loved one has moved on from another, but in this case, you did not develop a loving bond with her. Even though it is a tragic development you weathered it well enough that it did not cause you to be depressed over it. What did you do after that relationship, how did you move on?"

"That is when I met Toni."

Lisa: "Oh yes you mentioned Toni previously, The talker."

"I will pay for the pizza; would you walk with me for a while?" I need to clear this troubled head of mine. I have many more relationships to share with you. As you listen to me stories, you will see the evil within all of them."

148

The Evil Within Them

Lisa: "I will walk with you, in silence, no more conversation. You need quiet time to offload the memories you shared, or they will consume you."

We begin our walk around the block in total silence. I watch Lisa Walk away from me to smell the fragrance of lilies planted in a planter in front of a large building. I could not stop her in time or begin to warn her as she bent down placing her nose next to the yellow pedals. Just as she started to smell them, she realized they were fake. The look on her face was priceless. I started walking again in silence, when she caught up to me, she looked up at me with a dumb expression, did you see that? As we burst into laughter together.

We stayed silent, with no exchange of spoken words, continuing our walk back to her office.

Lisa: "No need to come into the office, thank you for the pizza and sharing a laugh about me smelling the plastic lilies. I knew they were fake; It was a test to see if you noticed."

149

The Evil Within Them

"If that's your story, then stick to it, see you next month."

With that admission, Lisa disappeared into her building. I turn away from the doorway to begin the solitary walk to my vehicle a few blocks away. I look up at the clouds on the western horizon, winter is approaching. I smell the moisture of impending rain.

As I walk alone, I recall the memories of good and tough times with everyone I have had the opportunity to meet in my life. Many of those memories now have tucked away forever. Therapy has helped to recall the lost ones. Those people had little to no impact on my life as they quickly faded as fast as they entered my life.

The best decision I ever made was to still be silent. I have nothing to prove to anyone nor do I need to convince anyone I am a great person. I cannot fix what I did not break, nor will I fight to keep someone who did not want to keep me. What they have done is on them. My only hope is that they do not regret their decisions. As for me, I am at peace with who I am.

The memories of the ones I truly, deeply loved are the ones I will never forget.

The Evil Within Them

Session Nine

I have arrived in Columbia, South Carolina once again to meet with the therapist. Lisa is waiting for my return.

I sat quietly in my car recalling a quote from Ernest Hemmingway.

"He once said*: In our darkest moment, we do not need solutions or advice, what we yearn for is simply human connection-a quiet presence, a gentle touch. These small gestures are the anchor that holds us steady when life feels like too much. Please do not try to fix me or take on my pain or push away my shadows. Just sit beside me while I work through my own inner storms. Be the steady hand I can reach for as I find my way. My pain is mine to carry, my battles mine to face alone. But your presence reminds me I am not alone in this vast, sometimes frightening world. It is a quiet reminder that I am worthy of love, even when I feel broken. So, in those dark hours when I lose my way, will you be here? Not to rescue me but as a companion. Hold my hand until dawn arrives, helping me remember my strength. Your silent support is the most precious*

The Evil Within Them

*gift you can give. It is love that helps me remember who
I am.*

Even when I forget."

I begin my walk to Lisa's office. I walk past the empty reception desk once occupied by an old lady, now retired a few months prior. Knocking on Lisa's door I hear the faint voice of "Please come in."

Lisa: "Hello Michael. You know the routine, have a seat anywhere you choose."

"There are only two choices Lisa I exclaim."

Lisa: "At least you have options Michael. I must apologize after our last visit I forgot to thank you for the pizza."

"Must have been the fragrance of the plastic flowers that clouded your brain functions."

The Evil Within Them

Lisa: "I did not need a reminder, but I do not recall the flowers had any fragrance." Now what would you like to discuss today?"

"Childhood, my father and a little about my mother. Not exactly in that order."

"I will begin with my father. There is not a lot of information in my memory about him when I was younger than thirteen or fourteen years old. He was in the AirForce, S.A.C Command for most of those early years. If he was not in a secured room watching radar screens, he was on a bomber flying cross country cheating on my mother. When he did come home, he was a mean man.

I am sure it was his demeanor and not from military training, although some of his tactics of discipline gave me insights into his reasoning for delivering corporal punishment on us.

Lisa: "Explain your last statement about the corporal punishment if you will, with additional details."

155

The Evil Within Them

As I mentioned it was either him or the training that prompted his thinking. You see in the military if someone got out of line. It was protocol to gather everyone in the platoon or the entire company to administer corrective action. You never singled out the source of who caused a problem, it was everyone's problem and everyone received punishment. The reasoning behind this is that the ones not involved in the dirty deed would find a way to correct the troublemaker.

This procedure to punish all instead of one spilled over to the children. Usually, my older brother's stupidity caused my father to not only punish my brother, but he also included my sister and I in the punishment."

Lisa: "What form of punishment did he use on the three of you?"

"It was always the belt across our butts as he instructed us to bend over a bed while he beat us uncomfortable. If it was not his belt he enjoyed slapping us across our head with his open hand.

The Evil Within Them

"I hated that man. I did not fear him, I just hated him."

One evening my father was upset at my brother for not feeding the animals correctly. I do not recall why, but my father once again thought it was a suitable action to slap my brother as punishment. That was a bad Idea on his part. You see my brother matured faster than I did. He was more muscular and taller than my father.

As soon as the hand hit my brother's face, the punching bag became my father's head. I hated when my mother came outside to break up the fight. I was hoping he would make up for the damage my father's belt did to my rear end.

Lisa: "How did your father react to that?"

"The good this is my father did have a few brain cells left to consider not doling out that type of punishment."

"He never hit either of us again."

The Evil Within Them

Lisa: "Do you have something to share about your mother?"

My mother was her glue that kept everything sane. She worked as an accountant for a shipping company in Tampa. When we got home from school, she would call the house and tell one of us what and how to cook dinner for the family. That is how I learned to cook. I was the only one to answer the phone when she called in the dinner recipe. I figured I was the dumb one to answer the phone. My siblings never answered the phone after they figured out what my mother was up to.

Lisa: "You have written a note in your questionnaire to ask about a deep fryer but did not give details."

"Lisa, what I am about to say can create an emotional response so, be prepared. Where is the tissue?"

Lisa: "Beside the chair to your right om the credenza. Please take your time."

158

The Evil Within Them

"It was springtime 1957. Bozier City, Louisianna. I am not exactly confident I received a true recall of the events that unfolded that day, I can only tell you the details of the event as described to me by my mother.

Lisa: "I see you are pausing, take a deep breath, continue when you are ready."

Tears are forming in my eyes as I struggle to control the emotions of what I am about to say to Lisa.

"I was a year and a half old, still crawling along the floor. My mother was in the kitchen cooking. I am not sure what it was, she never mentioned that detail. It is a hole in her story I believe.

"She.....

I pause again, grabbing more tissues.

159

The Evil Within Them

Lisa: "Take a breath I am not here to judge you, whatever it is, I can tell this is huge, you need to let it out."

My mother was frying food in a small deep fryer. When she finished frying the food she unplugged the fryer and let the electric cord drop off the edge of the counter. It did not have an on or off switch to control it.

I crawled into the kitchen, exploring the dangling cord, I pulled on the end of the cord bringing the hot oil contents in the deep fryer it down on me."

The hot oil landed on my let arm and legs.

I burned skin and the scars are still visible to remind me of that tragic event.

All my life, when someone sees the scars, I have had to explain the details of how this happened to me.

Lisa: "I am so sorry that happened to you. Can you shed some light on how this affected you? Specifically with the relationships you have had?" Did anyone ever express an unwillingness to date you because if the scars?"

"Yes, although not often. No one knows unless about them until I take off my shirt or drop my pants to be intimate. When the scars are exposed to the eye it is either acceptable or shocking. have to inquire. I am so, used to them being there I forget to mention them to the women I date. They feel sorry for me and stay long enough to get what they want from me, then find some-one who has nicer skin.

I tend to shy away from public swimming pools or private parties where I would have to wear a bathing suit. My wife never mentioned them in conversation. I recently posed the question to her; did she ever feel my scars were an issue to her at any time during our mar-riage together? She replied, she never gave them any thought and was never an issue to her.

My daughter occasionally lifts my shirt sleeve to look at my arm, although she has never commented negatively.

The Evil Within Them

It is extremely difficult to discard the thoughts my scares may have played some part in the failures of my relationships."

"No one has ever personally revealed this very theory directly to me, I know in my heart they cannot bear the burden of revealing the truth of their decision to move on."

"I just know it to be true."

Lisa: "How did you remain married if you feel this way? The scars had no bearing on your marriage, or did they? Did your stepson mention them in heated discussions or use the mentioning of them to you to hurt your feelings?"

"That was one place he never ventured. It would have been severely detrimental if he tried that dialogue on me. He realized that was a subject that would have triggered a response he did not want to deal with. Some things are out of bounds."

The Evil Within Them

Lisa: "I understand saying this to me today was a big step. Do you blame your mother for the accident somehow?"

"I have never once considered holding my mother accountable for her actions that day. It was an accident; I was supposed to be in another room. She never saw me crawl into that kitchen. My entire family of aunts and uncles never spoke about it. It was, simply accepted as an accident."

"I am the one who has had to live with it all my life."

"Not them"

Lisa: "Tragic events happen to people all over the world Michael. What I can tell you is this. The scars you carry are not only superficial but emotional scars of the event that day. You may never blame anyone or ask your mother for accountability, nevertheless her action was careless and should have been more thoughtful of the cord dangling from the counter knowing she had a baby in the house. I do not see what she was thinking."

"Lisa, remember it was 1957, back then the child awareness teachings we have today were nonexistent. I carry the burden of my actions that day, every day."

"No one else."

Lisa: "I am sorry I got, carried away with that. Our session has expired. I hope this session does not deter you from returning, you have a lot on your mind, and we will get it all on the table eventually. Goodbye for now,"

"See you next month, I will return."

Again, I leave Lisa's office to make the long walk to the parking garage in solitude. This time my mind does not wander in thought, I am silent. As I walk, I see familiar faces, I do not know, they walk the same path, except.

164

The Evil Within Them

My path…… is my life.

Everyone I encounter in my life; everyone I pass on the street can see the expression I have on my face.

No one sees the smile I have on the inside.

No one sees the physical or emotional scars I have carried with me; my entire life.

Reaching my vehicle, I stop while I momentarily reflect on Lisa's closing statement, remembering a Buddhist proverb.

Forgiveness does not mean you accept what they did. It means what happened, does not control you anymore.

The Evil Within Them

Session Ten

Lisa: "Good morning, Michael. How was your walk into the office today?

"Great, how are you today?

Lisa: "I am fantastic. This is our tenth session. In this session, I ask my clients if there is anything you need to discuss from our previous sessions you may have omitted, forgotten to mention or need to clarify today. Do you have anything to add?"

"No, I do not. What I have told you so far does not need revising or re-visiting memories filled away years ago. Recalling them once is enough and will only cause more pain for me. I have closed those chapters of my life."

Lisa: "Perfect, that is the answer I am looking for when I ask that question. It means you are progressing. So, without further ado. What would you like to discuss today?"

"Let us dive into some relationships that have caused more emotional concern than the scars on my body. I carry more scars than the ones you can physically see.

I have four women who have had a significant impact on my self-worth when it comes to having a relationship.

I will clarify; Not all my relationships were troubled or doomed by evil behavior. Some were very pleasant to be with. One of my sister's besties was so beautiful and gentle on my soul.

That changed when my parents signed me up for the Merchant Mariners academy in Baltimore, Maryland. So, that was an amicable split. There are more, I just do not recall all of them due to the insignificance of those relationships.

After I gained control of my restaurant, I started dating again. One lady in particular was a therapist for the public school system. Yes Lisa, I dated a therapist.

The Evil Within Them

My first encounter with a Pollyanna as she described herself. A terminology from Sigmund Freud's research on personality behavior.

I will refer to her with her initials only as 'KA.' An extremely attractive lady with beautiful hair. I have always been drawn to people with higher intellectual knowledge. She fits well in this category."

Lisa: "How did you two meet?"

"This will sound conceited, but it always begins the same Lisa; women are interested as soon as they see me. I happened to be at the restaurant one evening sitting at the counter. She is a customer, then she decides to sit next to me and strike up a conversation.

Immediately I loved her beauty and articulation. Not long afterwards, we exchange phone numbers, and one thing leads to the other. We begin to have dinner together on a regular basis. Albeit the evenings together were for food, cocktails with an occasional night of dancing to music. The Southern gentleman that I am, required me pick her up at her apartment, then select one of our favorite restaurants. Being the man, in her

169

life she determines I should pay for our nights out. I am the man she used for dinner, more on that later in my story."

Lisa: "You say that with a connotation I do not understand." 'What is the meaning behind that last statement?

"More clarity as I get further into the timeline. You see we, well, I thought we were dating. We were together a lot. I had no reason to believe there was anyone else in her life, except me.

That thought quickly began to fade when I received a warning shot across the bow.

One evening we were dinning out, when the owner of an Italian restaurant we frequented pulled me aside to divulge knowledge of specific behavior I needed to know about "KA." It was a warning that triggered embedded instincts. The wakeup calls so to speak.

It was time to ask questions during our next outing together."

The Evil Within Them

Lisa: "What did he tell you? What type of behavior was she engaged in?"

"Miss "KA" held an evil side to her. Unrecognized at the time. Now, here is the clarification I promised. After dinner, I would accompany her on a walk around the city, just a walk, we never held hands, we never kissed, even when we said goodbye to each other, and went our separate ways. I figured she was being cautious or a germaphobe. My emotions were in check at the time, especially after my divorce, I was not sure if I wanted a developing relationship anyway. Eventually she drew me in with the three words we all want to hear from a partner."

The, "love you" words.

"That kickstarted my feelings for her which upped the ante. The information received had been an isolated thought, not too sure of how I felt hearing this from her. It eventually triggered an unwelcome reaction when the slightest increase in moving forward with a more committed relationship was constantly deflected.

The Evil Within Them

We never went further than a night out for dinner and conversation.

Although she continued saying "Love you" to me every time we parted for the night or the ending to a text stream. I surmise when she conveyed it. It had a different meaning than when I said it to her.

You can love a car, your house, or a dog for that matter, but to be 'IN' Love is another level. Her level of love was meaningless. As time went on and on, for a year and a half, nothing changed in the relationship. I seriously took stock of the situation between us, becoming aware her feelings toward me were significantly nonexistent. It was the ruse she played with precise conclusions, not only while she was with me but with others.

Lisa: "Go on, I want to hear this. What do you mean when you said, "with others?"

"What I found strange with 'KA" was, she never wanted to go out of town with me. If she planned a trip it was always her going out of town. She booked trips everywhere. This was like a magician disappearing

172

behind a sheet or a wall. One evening enjoying a dinner with 'KA' we were, joined by one of her close friends as we were leaving the restaurant. Her girlfriend turns to say goodbye and mentioned a well to do party was occurring the next night. She suggested to 'KA" she should ask me to accompany her to the party. I can still recall how "KA" calmly answered her 'friend' The answer was a classic example of the technique she used to maintain control of the situation.

"KA" calmly said to her friend.

"You know it's an invitation only party and I do not think it would be appropriate to bring an uninvited guest."

"Before you ask a question about that statement, Lisa, let me clarify. I honestly felt relieved I was not on the list of attendees. Neither woman made any reference to who was hosting the party. Again, the shroud of secrecy prevailed with both of them."

"With the up-to-date information from the bird who landed on my shoulder. I had no choice but to skillfully try to interrogate her while we were together. This would be no easy task; she has a higher IQ than most people I knew. Now, keep this in mind. "KA" was incredibly careful when it came to using proper names of people she used as her source during our conversations. I knew they were the same people I knew or interacted with as a businessperson, except her engagements with them were quite different. She used reference points like the name of a business to describe her outings with them, never using given names.

At this point, there were subtle clues she unknowingly provided to piece together timelines of her daily routine to which systematically unraveled the game she played. The one-thousand-piece puzzle was forming before my eyes.

Lisa: "Oh tell me more, the recorder is on."

"My first encounter with a manipulative narcissist. Her college education enabled her to use the information she learned of how a narcissist operates willfully and skillfully with strategic precision of a skilled brain surgeon. Except she played with your mind instead of operating on it. I knew of the narcissist terminology but never felt the need to research information into this type of modeled human behavior.

"KA" was a professional when she wanted or needed something from an individual she deemed a source. She was well educated on the subject of narcissism and used this education in her dating career to gain everything she desired. One note to add. "KA" never once used her assets to influence a man's decision to provide for her. It was all mind manipulation. We all fell victim to her at some point."

Lisa: "ALL" you said ALL!"

"Oh yes. A lot of us. She used me for dinner, she used another guy for her lunch, she used another friend for breakfast. Every one of us received the same attention, which trapped us in her web of deceit. She used a tactic I call devoted attention by slightly caressing a source's leg or arm with her hand when seated next to each other at a bar or table. It was the use of her misguided affection to gain control of you. This sultry erotic behavior-initiated temptation to the very the core

175

of our adulthood, we just misunderstood the intention of that kindness."

"My awakening finally arrived.

Her playground now exposed, I no longer desired to be her playmate. Figuring out her operation would have taken a little longer if I had not received the information from my friend, I admit being blindsided by my emotional love for her. To halt the game, I simply quit taking her out."

Lisa: 'What did she do then, you must have been emotionally hurt when you discovered what she was about?"

"Not so much. I was not fully involved with her emotionally. I will repeat, there was no intimacy during the relationship, not even a kiss on the lips. She was incredibly careful to keep her sources at a predetermined distance, along with everyone else she played with. Looking back on my time with her and now fully educated with knowledge of narcissistic behavior, it all makes perfect sense of what she did and how she did it.

The Evil Within Them

She never believed, I or the others would ever catch on to her plan."

Lisa: "How so?"

"I will say this again."

"KA" kept all of her men friends strategically close enough to ensure they were, connected to her with enough emotional dedication to continue seeing her. She was incredibly beautiful and articulate. She drew clear boundaries to maintain a diversion without getting fully committed. When someone made a move to get closer or showed signs of wanting to initiate intimacy, she would disappear from their life long enough to calm the storm, then resurface back into their life to restart the connection again. She repeated this protocol repeatedly with me."

"I became frustrated after a year and a half of playing her game of catch and release. It was not like I did not have the sixth sense to know what was happening. The relationship was always one sided. I continued to play along just to be with her. I decided it was time to stop making any effort to see her.

177

The Evil Within Them

It is not the person I needed to let go of it, it is the idea of who I thought she was. I needed to reclaim my self-worth; when I stopped playing the game it ended for her.

She moved onto another source for dinner and conversation. It is unfortunate this man was a long-term lawyer friend of mine. I could not bear to warn him; he needed some company to help him regain his man card. He struggled to find a suitable partner as well as I did and who is better to have with you than a narcissist with personality disorders.

Sadly, I report his encounter with her ended just as mine did. I do believe she played with him longer than with me. He often frequents the restaurant my daughter now owns. He does not speak of her unless I inquire. He is a changed man."

"I want to share a meme I read on a social media platform site that read:"

"*She was never yours. It was just your turn.*"

The Evil Within Them

Lisa: "We have to cut short today. I have a doctor's appointment I need to attend. Do you have any final comments before we end?"

"Yes, I remember a conversation we had over the phone. "KA" wanted to discuss the contraction of herpes simplex, going on for an hour about the disease referring to a "friend' had recently discussed with her in therapy. I realized after our call ended, she used the terminology, "friend" to actually mean herself. I felt deeply sorry for her as it opened my eyes to why she never initiated intimacy with me or anyone else she used during the course of her life.

"The evil within them always comes out."

"I will see you next month."

The Evil Within Them

Session Eleven

Lisa: "We meet again Michael. How have you been? Why are you late? You are never late to your appointments."

"Long slow walk from the garage today. There is ice on the sidewalk. I watched a couple of people slip and fall, then I helped an elderly lady to cross the street."

Lisa: "What a gentleman." I have snow boots today for that very reason. So, you mentioned there are four women you dated that influenced you. The last one you covered well enough. That leaves three left. Which one would you like to discuss next?"

"I will keep them in the order they entered and exited my life."

Lisa: "Ok, who is next then?"

The Evil Within Them

Once again, I will use her initials. "KD"

Lisa: "Like 'KA' this lady is now; KD?" Did I hear you correctly?"

"Did you start the Bluetooth recorder?"

Lisa: "I did."

"After I finished with "KA" I found myself heading out to dinner by myself. The usual Thursday, Friday, and Saturday nights. I have a taste for fine establishments for dining out. Junk food chain restaurants are not on this list. I frequented several restaurants, I knew the owners and trusted the chefs to provide delicious food."

"I returned to Casa Bella, the Italian place I mentioned before. I liked Joe. He made every effort to come sit with me and enjoy a beer together while we watched tv at his bar. If you ever visit Aiken, South Carolina, give the place a try. The food is excellent."

Lisa: "I will, but am I not here to discuss your relationship issues? Is there a point you are going to include with the plug you mentioned?"

"Yes, Lisa, please, be patient with me?

"I also frequented a steakhouse called Prime Steak. These two are the only restaurants I chose for my dining experience."

Lisa: "Ok I get it"

"It may have been six month or so of eating out. It was again another weekend alone. I wanted a fillet and chose Prime that night. Randy was a dear friend. We were like brothers from another mother. Yes, that is a Southern cliché.'

"I sat at the bar talking to Randy, eating my dinner. The conversation centered on a recent fishing trip.

183

The Evil Within Them

We booked the Checa Lodge & spa. Islamorada in the Florida Keys."

"This place was fantastic."

Lisa: "I am failing to see your point in relation to the direction of our session."

"Lisa, chill out, I am getting to the point of my story.

"The first fishing trip was with two other men friends we knew from Aiken. While we were discussing the latest trip. I could not help but notice an attractive woman behind me having dinner with a girlfriend. She stood up to leave and approached Randy to politely thank him for the meal and give him a hug as she left.

Randy knew of my situation with 'KA' I had already filled him in on the details of why I was now single again.

"KD' had now left the building. We finished watching her walk out without breaking our necks."

Randy turns to me and asks If I would like to go out with her, mentioning he would contact her to ask for me. I simply replied with, "You can give her my phone number anytime, and thank you."

It would not be prudent to turn down an opportunity to date such a beautiful woman. I slapped Randy on the back shoulder after I paid my tab and exited the building. I am assured no one stared at my backside like every man in Prime did that night 'KD' walked out ahead of me."

Lisa: "What a great friend to help set you up with a high caliber woman. You must have been on top of the world at that moment."

"Honestly, I never gave it another thought."

Lisa: "Why. Did you lose faith in her calling you? Were you sure Randy gave out your number?"

"He did. About a week later the phone rang from an unknown number. It was 'KD.' We spoke for an hour in what seemed like the longest job interview I ever had. But in the end, we agreed to meet back at Prime for

185

dinner to further the conversation and get to know each other.

We agreed to start dating from that point on for eight months."

Lisa: "Eight months, which was significantly shorter than 'KA' what happened in that period that caused the short romance to deteriorate?"

"It was the experience of dating 'KA' and a few others before her that instilled the caution necessary to deal with 'KD.'

'Although extremely attractive, I saw the pattern repeating itself."

Lisa: "You are smarter now? You have seen this picture before?"

"Yes, a few times before. I was living in a small apartment close to the restaurant. My ex-wife had not transferred the house to me at this time of dating 'KD.' Our relationship strengthened, unlike 'KA,' 'KD' had

186

no problem using her assets to manipulate the relation-ship."

"I became a nightly resident in her bed. This may be too much information, but you need to under-stand what transpired."

Lisa: "Hold on I am getting some popcorn out of the microwave. Wait here."

"Are you joking Lisa? You cannot be serious?"

Lisa: "Yes I am joking, please continue."

"Here goes. Wait a minute. Do you really need to record this part?"

Lisa: "It is for training purposes only"

"Oh, I am calling B.S. on that statement Lisa, you have no employees." Anyway, here goes nothing. We became intensely intimate within a brief time. Every night we were together, we were intimate, like all night, three am intimate. I taught her a few tricks and she taught me a few in return. It was nonstop. Sometimes I had to beg her to stop and let me get a few hours of sleep before I needed to go start up the restaurant the next morning.

Lisa is eyes wide open after listening to me declare the last piece of information, but this is something she needed to know to grasp the reality I lived with. Her glare is that of a deer in the headlights.

I snap my fingers to bring her back to me. Lisa explodes on me.

Lisa: "WHAT DID YOU JUST DO?"

"I snapped my fingers at you."

Lisa momentarily covers her face with both hands. Releasing them instantly to reply."

The Evil Within Them

Lisa: "I deserved that. Please continue. Not with that story, move on from that please, more information on the relationship and less on the intimate details.

"Gladly. But, this is therapy, I am supposed to tell you the details, including the deep dark secrets.

Lisa has a dismal look on her face, then waves her hand in the air without saying a word.

I continue.

I will refrain from those details, here is where the manipulative behavior begins. 'KD' drove a Jaguar. She begins with the sob story of how the car is giving her trouble and needs replacement, with a newer model.

I now know how the narcissist begins with gaslighting. This may take some time before the source starts believing what they are told. This usually triggers the sources' mind to comply with the narcissist's desires.

'Remember, they always begin with a convincing story.'

To support her need for a new vehicle, she would search online every evening, usually while I lay in bed next to her at night looking at new and used BMW's or Mercedes vehicles. Always showing me her selection and asking me my opinion of this or that car and the color she picked out. I would reply with kind words; I figured out the game too soon but played the game just as well as she did. The amazing thing is she never followed through on a purchase with her own credit or money.

The day came when her Jaguar was gone and in dire need of personnel transportation. "KD" provided explanation or understanding of how the car disappeared. She made a request to "borrow" my five series BMW. I briefly inquired about the cars' whereabouts and received a fictitious rambling story. Being the perfect gentleman always helping a damsel in distress. I handed over my keys with the understanding I was "loaning her my car." This left me without a vehicle. Nothing to worry about, I lived in close proximity and could walk to the restaurant to work.

Lisa: "Let me guess she kept the car too long? Did she swindle you out of your car, didn't she?"

The Evil Within Them

"Yes, she did. I was walking to work, in the South Carolina summer heat. It was under a mile, but I was soaking wet from sweat when I arrived. To cool my body, I would unlock the front door and head for the walk-in cooler to bring down my body temperature. Later on in the relationship, I found out her last boy-friend paid for the Jaguar, and he demanded she return it, when he discovered she left him for me. It was a demand she had to comply with, or he would have it re-possessed."

She continued bringing cars to me to evaluate and determine if they were worth purchasing. At first, I figured she required my opinion, then I figured out the scheme she was playing out. You see, bringing the vehicles to me for my inspection was not her intention. It turned out she was hoping I would eventually cave in and buy the car for her. I was not as rich and famous as she thought. I admit she was great in bed but not that good."

Lisa: "Michael! That is inappropriate." Continue please."

The Evil Within Them

"I will not apologize; this is a paid session, correct?"

Lisa reluctantly nods her head, and I continue with my session.

"Her attempts to manipulate the relationship did not stop there. I planned to take her on one of the fishing trips to Islamorada, but with other good fellows in attendance, it made better sense to plan a vacation week with her in Charleston, South Carolina at the Market Pavilion, concierge level. It was the start of the Spoleto festival of artist, craft vendors and theatrical shows.

Lisa: "That must have been a great weekend with her?" I would love to see my husband book a trip to Charleston."

"I do not think you would be so evil to him like she did with me. Please reserve your judgement until I explain the evil trick she played out after we left Aiken."

Lisa: 'Oh no, I knew this part was too good to be true."

"Since "KD" was still using my BMW, the plan was for her to pick me up at my apartment and we would drive to Charleston together.

Lisa: "What happened on the way down to Charleston?"

"You are going to love this part of my session today."

"I diligently awaited her arrival with a single day bag. Men do not pack a big suitcase. I waited on the front porch of the old antebellum home where I rented a room."

193

The Evil Within Them

"I watch the white BMW five series pull into the circular driveway, the pebbles crunching under to rotating wheels as the car comes to a full stop. Naturally, I ask her to pull the lever to open the trunk before exiting the driver's seat. Exiting the driver's door, she ignores my request and proceeds to walk around the car, standing next to the passenger side door, waiting for her southern gentleman to gallantly open the door for her.

I open the door like a good boy, and she replies that trunk space is full, suggesting I should lay my bag on the back seat. "You see, opening the trunk would allow me to place my day bag in the trunk alongside her luggage. I obviously am not thinking clearly, I have been diligently waiting on the porch in the South Carolina summer heat. I willfully agreed without discussion or question, placing my bag in the back seat, behind the driver's side."

Lisa" "Seams legit. But I can guess this story gets even better?"

"Patience Lisa, the good part is coming."

194

The Evil Within Them

"I begin our two-and-a-half-hour drive to Charleston, South Carolina As I drive, we are conversing together on a number of subjects, "when," we get halfway to Charleston, she turns to me with a concerned look on her face, promptly asking me to stop the car. Once we were, fully stopped, she declares.

"I think I forgot to put my suitcases in the trunk."

"Further requesting I exit the car to confirm the whereabouts of her luggage."

"If looks could do damage, this was one of those occasions. I stood at the back of my car staring into an empty trunk space. Re-entering the driver's seat, I acknowledged her luggage was not stowed in the trunk. She then proceeds with two options, the first being, drive all the way back to Aiken, South Carolina, second option, we could continue to Charleston where she, I said SHE, would buy herself a new wardrobe."

"Remember that last statement, Lisa."

Lisa: "Ok I will remember. Which option did you choose?"

195

The Evil Within Them

"With an affirming kiss and her hands delicately placed in the right spot, I continued to Charleston, I will give you three guesses who bought the clothes, but the first two guesses do not count. She also needed a toothbrush and toothpaste. I made her buy that at Walmart with her own money. She did not forget her purse.

One footnote to the trip. She had stuffed her makeup bag on the floorboard behind the passenger seat out of plain sight. I refrained from questioning its magical appearance in the hotel room shortly after checking in."

Lisa: "How much did this trip cost you?"

"More than I anticipated. When we returned to Aiken, I followed her upstairs to her bedroom for one last invitation before leaving. It was no surprise to me to find her empty suitcase, sitting on the chase lounge in her bedroom. She never packed it with clothes nor intended to bring it with her, her ruse now exposed in full view.

The Evil Within Them

Lisa: "Did you break up after that? I could never conceive of such a plan. I think my husband would have left me on the highway if I told him to stop and look in the trunk."

"No, I continued for a little while longer in the relationship but, she quit the shenanigans. There were no more games played no more gaslighting. I did not buy her a car and finally got mine back when she got her ex-husband to buy one for her. She Knew 'KA' well enough and tried to copy the same protocol with her men. The only problem is, I had a year and a half of experience and training on sleight magic tricks.

Lisa: 'Her ex bought her a car?"

"She was good at manipulating him somehow. I am sure she used her assets to secure a seven series BMW." Of course, the car arrived after we broke up."

The Evil Within Them

Lisa: "What did you like about 'KD'? Did you love her?

"She was the first woman since my divorce and the first woman I dated that held me close at night. She was also the first woman to acknowledge I had blue eyes. She was also the first women ever to tell me wonderful things to me. She knew how to use flattering statements in order to manipulate the relationship. She gave me the type of intimacy I lacked in my marriage.

Lisa: 'Interesting, elaborate on the things she said to you. Was this during intimacy or in general?

"In general conversation, she praised me a lot with affirming words like, how handsome I was. This captured my heart; no woman shared such affection towards me, including my wife of twenty-four years. This behavior was new to me; I had never experienced hearing affectionate words from anyone during any previous relationship."

The Evil Within Them

"Other than the few attempts to manipulate me, we had a wonderful time together. I always suspected she was seeing her ex-husband the high school sweetheart while we were together. The clues were everywhere."

Lisa: "It sounds like you did have feelings for her. She provided the comfort you were missing in other relationships. How and why did you suspect she was seeing her ex?"

"She somehow acquired two condominiums in Hilton Head Island. Those are not cheap."

Lisa: "What broke you two up?

"We were out at Prime having dinner one night. A handsome man came to the table to talk directly to her. He had some balls to approach the table and begin talking to her, not me, not us, just her. The crazy thing is his girlfriend was there with him. He left her at the bar to talk to 'KD.'"

The Evil Within Them

"Later on, I discovered she started a relationship with him. I also found out she enticed him to come to the table that night. Another woman leaving me for another man."

Lisa: "That was the end of that relationship for sure." Why do you think she left you for him?"

"Money, plain and simple she was a gold digger looking for a stable revenue source. When that man told his story of being a professional harness racer. It sealed the deal for her, she fell head over heels for him.

I have no regrets; I had an enjoyable time with her." I will admit, I went into a depressive state of mind after that. That break up hurt to the very core of my soul. The was first woman I felt 'In love' although she maintains he love was real. I doubt it existed in reality. I lost eighteen months of my life.

Lisa: "That is the first time you have expressed the emotion of 'In Love' in any of our sessions. Did you honestly feel that for her?"

The Evil Within Them

"Absolutely, we still communicate often with each other."

Lisa: "That concludes our session for this month. Same time next month? It should have warmed up enough to melt the ice off of the sidewalks but be careful walking to the parking garage."

"Absolutely"

The Evil Within Them

Session Twelve

I enter the downtown garage turnstile, purchase my parking ticket, and drive up a few decks to find an empty space. I take a moment to finish listening to Bon Jovi, "Living on a prayer" as loud as I can stand it. One of the most iconic songs of his career. I step out of the garage into the warming sunlight. It is now March, the beginning of the warming trend in South Carolina. I am in an upbeat mood, especially after listening to music. I will be discussing one of the longest running relationships after being divorced. Albeit off and on with her, it was another episode I will never forget.

I enter Lisa's office without saying hello, I find the chair in front of her desk and place myself in a comfortable position. Lisa once again is displaying her Chesser Cat smile, no words just her smile.

"Yes, Lisa, I have noticed you painted the drab off white walls with a nice lite blue, thank you for not choosing pink! I know you women love to have everything pleasingly PINK!

203

The Evil Within Them

Lisa: "I thought you might like it. Thank you for expressing your opinion so eloquently. Let me start the reorder and you can begin anytime you are ready. What, or who in your successive line of women would you like to discuss today?"

"I seem to have touched the ugly nerve within you, please put it back where it was, and I will do the same. I mean no offense to my opening statement, so, let us start over, I will start as soon as you punch the button on the recorder."

Lisa: "We will agree to disagree. Begin please."

"The relationship I will describe today spanned a period of six years; it was an off and on scenario. I may require another session to disclose the full details of my time with her."

Lisa: "Six years? It is ok with me if you need more than one session express your feelings about her. What initials shall we give this one?"

204

The Evil Within Them

"JJ"

Lisa: "Interesting, how did you meet "JJ?"

"This story begins a long time ago. You see, "JJ" was married to one of my best friends. First I have to tell you about him. He was the type of person who never met a stranger, a continually active man with extreme generosity and the IQ of a genius. He wore cowboy hats the matching boots. This man could talk to a total stranger for five minutes and immediately welcomed into their inner circle. He shook your hand with the strength of a bull. You knew he was serious when you met him. It was his signature card he carried with him.

"When those two invited you to a party at their house, you did not say no or make an excuse for not attending. The attendees were a whos' who of Aiken.

"There was a time period in life where my wife and I sold our restaurant in Aiken to a neighbor and moved to Fripp Island to live. I could operate my contracting business from anywhere. So, I thought. When we traded the restaurant for the beach house to regain

control of the restaurant. I let my wife operate the restaurant. I reached out to my best friend to see if his company needed any help."

"He went out of his way to secure me a position,
he was that kind of a man."

Lisa: "Very commendable of him."

Yes it was, unfortunately he struggled with hep-
atitis, contracted from a blood transfusion needed from
a sustaining injury in a horrific vehicle accident some
years prior. He was a few years older than me and his
wife. Eventually he contracted cancer and passed away.

"JJ" called to ask if I would be a pall bearer.
That is one man I was honored to carry to his resting
place."

Lisa: "Tragic story. How did "JJ" cope with his
loss?"

206

The Evil Within Them

"She was devastated at losing him. It was under-
standable to see her cry like she did. The funeral home
and grave side ceremony was attended by everyone in
Aiken. The procession needed a large police presence
for traffic control. My vehicle was the first one behind
the funeral director's limo. He was that close of a friend
to me.

Lisa: "I see, this was traumatic for you as well?"

"Indeed, it was, simply heartbreaking for me." I
have never had a friend like him and never will again."

Lisa: "Is this when you began dating "JJ" after
his funeral? Did you two like each other before his pass-
ing? Anything you need to share along those lines?"

"No, we were just friends, always friends.

Although soon after the funeral I received a call
from a mutual friend inquiring if I would reach out to
her. They informed me she had been lying in bed cry-
ing, refusing to get up. They asked If I would take her

out to dinner, just to get her out of the house. I agreed to be the guy.

I decided to reach out via text message, inquiring if she would consider going out with me for dinner. Immediately she accepted with conditions.

One. We were to do this as two friends having dinner and conversation with no other intentions or expectations.

Two. We need to pick a place discreet enough our outing would not be seen by anyone that may misunderstand the situation. Her concerns were easily addressed. She felt it was too early to proclaim she was moving on to another man so soon after her husband funeral.

"Being the gentleman I am this clearly made sense to me. So, we met at the "Variety" restaurant outside of town. We drove separately, entered the restaurant, and asked for a booth in the back room away from the main dining area. We sat across from each other ordering cocktails."

"I expected a somber women distraught with the loss of her companion, my close friend. The woman I met was so funny, joyous with jokes and laughter, not the later. The meeting turned into the happiest night I have had in several years with the women before her. They others never laughed this much at themselves much less a telling joke."

"The sun had set when we exited the restaurant with the parking lot dimly lit, I accompanied her to her car."

"Reaching the car, I attempted to open her door like a gentleman. I guess the cocktails had kicked in full swing when she turned around, threw her arms around my shoulders, and began a series of enthusiastic kisses. I was welcoming the embrace with every fiber of my being. She was the most beautiful woman I had ever been, attracted to. When I say beautiful I do not mean just her facial beauty. She had a beautiful soul as well."

"At least I thought so at that moment."

Lisa: "Oh no! Michael, you painted a pretty picture for me. How could this relationship turn on you?"

The Evil Within Them

"I thought I had stumble into the perfect relationship with the perfect companion. Although we kept the relationship a secret from everyone for six months before we decided to go public and tell our friends. A couple of girlfriends knew long before that."

"In the beginning and throughout the relationship, our time together, she initiated with a text or a phone call to come over for dinner, "JJ" was an excellent cook. None of the previous two women could or would cook for me. After dinner and "JJ" smoking a cigarette and drinking a couple cocktails we would head upstairs to her bedroom."

Lisa: "Do you need to give details of your intimate times together so. I can understand the gravity of your story?"

'It does make the story more interesting to know how she operated."

Lisa: "You mean manipulating you with her assets, not in an operational connotation. Correct?"

The Evil Within Them

"You would be correct in that assumption.

"She enjoyed the intimate moments as more than I did. Then we would lay in bed and watch tv and fall asleep in each other's arms. "JJ" gave me more of that close touchy-feely closeness I yearned for. I was in a lovely euphoric state of mind when I was with her.

We made up a word for it. We called it "twangling" together, a mix between together and entangled. I provide many nights of emotional support. Holding her in my arms for a year while she cried out for the loss of her husband and the emotional thoughts of thinking she was cheating on him. Even though he was gone from her life.

I never thought of her as a manipulator or a narcissist, "JJ" was the kindest woman, always holding me, touching me. It felt right being with her. Nothing was wrong we enjoyed each other. Our friends accepted our relationship, being convinced we were right for each other, My daughter accepted her.

Lisa: "Again Michael this is a beautiful love story. But you are here because something went wrong. What happened?

211

The Evil Within Them

Lisa: "You have stopped again. Are you trying to remember it correctly before speaking?"

"Yes" Give me a moment?"

"Any and all relationships begin the same way. In the beginning both participants represent themselves in their best behavior. After that the scenery changes too, I need this fixed; I need that repaired. I cannot afford a contractor. I seriously thought we were in love; I did use the word "WE" and "IN LOVE" actually I was deeply in love with her, she was not "IN LOVE" with me. I will say when you have that much intimacy together you fall down the rabbit hole quickly. My feelings for her were on a rocket ship to mars.

"The fairytale began unraveling after the first year. It was springtime. We were, invited to a friend's wedding reception at a local historical hotel, the "Wilcox" The wedding coincided with the spring running of the Kentucky Derby. Mint julips were handed out like glasses of water. "JJ" was, noticeably intoxicated and begins to fondle my crotch at the table in front of her sister and other guests."

212

The Evil Within Them

"Politely I lean over to whisper in her ear that people can see where she placed her hands. I merely wanted to slow her down until we could get back to her place. Unfortunately for me, I succeeded in awakening an evil monstrous vulgar slaughtering of my ego in front of everyone."

"She then left the table to go outside to smoke one of her cigarettes. I then acknowledged my respect to everyone and walked outside to meet with her in an attempt to calm the situation. To no avail I once again met with a volley of profanity. I then informed "JJ" she needed to secure transportation back to her house. The best thing I did that day was walk away from her, I was leaving the party."

"Now' I must add to one her leaving the table to step outside to smoke a cigarette. This was normal practice for her when we went to a fine restaurant. Although this smoke break began shortly after we seated at a fine restaurant. The very second the waitstaff placed her first cocktail on the table in front of her, she would retrieve a cigarette pouch from her purse, lift the cocktail in the other hand, declaring she was going outside to have a pre-dinner smoke.'

213

The Evil Within Them

'She left me sitting at the table by myself every time we went out until the food arrived. Then re-enter the restaurant to consume the meal. We exchanged veery little dialogue between us during the course of the night out."

"It was several days before she contacted me. I had no intention of reclaiming the relationship she destroyed that day. She had this plan to reunite with me. Her words comforted me. I caved; we began seeing each other again."

"Once again I performed a honeydew list of work at her house. I repaired her front door, ceiling fan replacement and provide help in fixing her BMW M3 rag top, readying it to sell."

"The house was, designed by her late husband. A beautiful two-story home with a large deck with a scenic view of a small pond from the back deck."

Lisa: "Sounds like a wonderful place. I want to touch on one aspect of your story today, you mentioned she left you inside at your table while she went out to smoke. Did you not think this was rude behavior?" Why did you allow this to happen?"

The Evil Within Them

"Good question, I admit I allowed it to continue without initiating a confrontation. Let the sleeping dog lay where he is, or you run the chance of getting bit."

Lisa: "You chose not to engage because it would cause her to release the evil within her? It was the best choice you could have made at the time. Please continue with your story."

"One day she asked if I could replace a couple of three-way switches on the ground level of her house. I attempted to research the brand of switch the building contractor used, which was no longer available and purchased switches I knew would work as a replacement. Long story made short and leaving out technical information no one would understand.

The existing switches installed by the original contractor were no longer available. So, I used newer modern electrical switches. Because she now had only one three-way switch instead of one at each wall, again the evil in her released a verbal assault targeting my ability as a man to fix the problem. I had enough of this

215

behavior towards me and left her for a second time with the intent to stay away for good. I was not going to accept this type of verbal abuse anymore.

Lisa: "She had hidden anger issues that inadvertently were, somehow triggered from time to time. You never know what it is that triggers someone's explosive behavior.

"Yes, this is true, what triggered these evil explosive responses left you in total disbelief of what caused the outburst in the first place. I constantly questioned my actions. Later on, I concluded it was her way of keeping me at a specific distance, not a physical distance mind you but an emotional distance. This was her means of manipulating and controlling our relationship.

Lisa: "Can you elaborate on that statement? Why would she use her anger issues to gain an advantage with your relationship with her? Did "JJ" not love you?

The Evil Within Them

"Good question Lisa, this is why I use you for therapy. You see, she always displayed her feelings of emotion, very caring, touchy feely, including verbal admonishment of the three words, "I Love You."

"One day we were on the subject of love and how much I loved her. I made the mistake of expressing, I was deeply "IN LOVE" with her. Her reply drove the nail into the coffin she used to destroy every deep emotion I had left for her. It was an awakening for me. My feelings were checked at the gate.

Her response opened the door for my eventual exit.

Lisa: "Did she explode on you in anger?"

"No, this time she calmly replied; I quote her saying,

Michael, I love you but, "I AM NOT IN LOVE WITH YOU."

Lisa: "You must have been devastated hearing this from her? Everything you have said sounded so perfect. What else did she say to you?

"She did provide an expanded explanation into why "we" did not share the same feelings. Her feeling of love was still rooted in the loss of her husband. Mine were, created by her interactions with me, as I mentioned she provided the type of contact I failed to receive from my marriage. I misunderstood her actions for love. She was performing   physical and emotional actions for her own needs as a woman. They were not to be, misconstrued as devoted love for me as a soul mate, she lost her soulmate, and I was merely a temporary replacement for dinner, bonding and intimacy, nothing more.

"Once again I made the mistake of believing I had found my soulmate for life. I never expected to hear the words she used during that conversation. That was one hell of a wakeup call for me that day.

Lisa: "Our normal one-hour session has concluded. My next appointment has cancelled so, I will allow you to stay a little longer if there is anything on your mind at the moment you need to share while it is fresh on your mind."

218

The Evil Within Them

"Yes I do have another story that rivals the one about the light switches. It just surfaced from my memory as I was speaking.

Period of time had passed when "JJ's" when my phone began to ring. It was "JJ." We had exchanged pleasantries when she revealed that she was invited to a Family wedding in Pennsylvania. One thing led to another, and I agreed to accompany her to the wedding. Of course I had to buy my own plane ticket. At least she bought her own. Once we arrived I was greeted by the family as if I had never left her side. She was embarrassed to tell them I was not in her life at the time."

"The reception was at a small outdoor venue with white tents and plenty of food. I watched couple after couple take a stroll around a lush green field. The next thing I knew, "JJ" asked me to walk with her around the field like the couples before us." We began the walk. I was a little surprised when "JJ" reached out to hold my hand, a few steps later snuggled in close to me, then she embraced me by wrapping her arms around my waist. We actually stopped engaging each other with an enthusiastic kiss. This suggestive interaction manufactured the feelings I have held at bay since our last breakup. My emotions soared high up to the clouds. I had a big smile on my face. She was back in my arms once again.

Lisa: "How nice of you to walk with her, how did this work out, I can assume she wanted to ask you to come back to her, since she asked you to walk with her. Often enough breakups reunite with better results. Did she ask you?

"Lisa. That was my very thought. So, halfway back to the tents, she said nothing about reuniting. So, I decided to ask her that very question when we were about fifty yards away from returning to the tents where everyone was standing."

Lisa: "Go on, I want to hear the end of this fairytale story before you leave today. What was her answer?"

"Do I need to actually spell it out for you?

Lisa: "YES! Michael."

The Evil Within Them

"The evil ego came roaring out of her. Thankfully, we were not inside the tent with everyone else. I had a sixth sense this would happen. I had a fifty-fifty chance of a roll of the dice, and I lost again. After her outburst of aggression, we returned to the tent, she left my side to talk to a family member. I walked straight thru the tent, out to the rental car to be alone."

"My self-esteem now crushed again. Later, I drove us back to the hotel, slept beside her in bed, then drove to the airport the next morning for the return flight. That entire time after the reception was in total silence with each other. We were now airborne, then for some reason I failed to understand, she unbuckled her seatbelt and curled up close to me, laying her head on my shoulders." It was not the embrace of love or affection a normal person with feelings, this was an embrace of sorrow for what she had done to me. It is her attempt to make me feel better. I could not make myself reciprocate, keeping my arms and hands to myself, I felt nothing but disgust for her. That was the longest plane ride home."

'I was ashamed of myself for letting her manipulate my feelings again. Landing back at Augusta international airport we retrieved our luggage and headed to her vehicle. She then drove me home to my house. I exited the vehicle, grabbed my luggage, and said goodbye."

"That was the single word I spoke to her since the walk in the field."

Lisa: "Obviously all she wanted was a temporary companion to be with her, she did not share the same feelings you possessed for her, you must have realized this by now?"

"You are exactly right. I was treated like a cinematic prop, discarded like one off use for a specific purpose. The only reason she asked me to attend, the family event, they all had significant others, she could not accept the thought of attending alone. Once again emotionally crushed.

Lisa: "I am sure you have many more stories to tell. But we are reserving them for another session if that is ok with you?"

222

"It is, I have to get out of here. I plan to treat myself to a steak dinner tonight. By myself, alone, with no drama."

See you next month, Lisa.

Another long drive back to Aiken, South Carolina, reflecting back on my sessions with Lisa. I remember more details about each story I should have revealed. Albeit some of the details of my life cannot be expressed in one session. The highlights of each will have to suffice for now.

I feel my energy returning with every session. Comparing therapy to a weightlifter. The more you lift, the stronger the muscles become, enabling you to lift the same weight, easier the next time.

The Evil Within Them

Session Thirteen

The forty-five minute drive to Columbia, South Carolina proved to be longer than the normal time it usually takes. I was not due to traffic conditions, just me and my thoughts. I have too many stories to present to my therapist. All of them mean something to me, all of my relationships begin to fail at some point. Is it me? I question this a lot. I realize I cannot manage or change the evil within them. Although this may be the factor to which draws me to them. These women were strong willed with determination to succeed beyond what a man can provide. The skilled prevail in life.

Once again I enter Lisa's office.

Lisa: "Hello Michael. What is on your mind today? Any reflection on our last session?

"I have nothing more to say about those episodes. I would like to move forward with more information on episodes with "JJ" but first I will tell you about "D."

225

The Evil Within Them

Lisa: "D"? Who is this?"

In the interim time period, I left "JJ" a friend asked me to consider a lady who recently became available, knew about my single status, and expressed some interest in me. We connected and after the initial interviewing process we made it official.

"D" had a completely different demeaner. She was a registered RN in a robotic surgery unit in Augusta, Georgia. Initially we grew emotionally connected. Although history repeats itself with me and relationships. She had three children, two were remarkably successful with one son addicted to drugs.

Lisa: "I see a pattern coming, what happened to this relationship?"

"Let me tell you the good parts before I get to the bad stuff, LISA!"

"Again, excessive use of alcohol ruins it for me every time. She slept at my house every night while we

226

were together. I welcomed her nightly companionship but then realized she used me for comfort very differently than the others. I soon concluded her sleepovers were not because of her love for me. She needed a secure place to live because of her son's drug addiction activities. She was so afraid a dealer would break in at night to kill her and her son for the money he owed them.

One time the police broke her door down at three am, with a warrant based on an anonymous tip, her house was a drug lab. They pulled her out of bed placing her in handcuffs. Keep in mind she sleeps naked.

Lisa: "Did they allow her to put clothes on?"

They gave her a tee shirt to wear. I assumed staying at my house gave her a secure place to lay her head and the warmth of a companion. I knew there was no emotional connection developing between us. She was another woman in my life with a need to feel secure.

227

The Evil Within Them

Lisa: "Oh wow. What would happen between you two?

"We went snow skiing in Colorado with her sister, father, and stepmother. It was a week couped up in a small efficient apartment on the side of a ski resort.

All she did was drink wine, read a book, drink more wine while ignoring me. I could not wait to get back to South Carolina.

That was another lesson I learned. Now back to "JJ." We were not together at the time I was dating "D" when my cell phone rang with the familiar tone I selected for "JJ," it was a request to come over for dinner and an afternoon delight. I knew better than to be set up and accept the invitation, so when she back called asking my ETA, I informed her I was in a committed relationship at the time and seeing her while attached to "D" was unethical.

"JJ" thought she had the power to pull me away from a committed relationship with "D." Albeit a rocky one, I declined the invitation she extended for an evening of dinner and afternoon delight. I have no apologies for spoiling her evening plans. That ruined her ego.

228

The Evil Within Them

Lisa: "JJ" knew you were seeing "D" Why would "JJ" ask you to cheat on "D" like that? So nonchalant? Obviously, she thought she had power over you, and you would accept her invitation."

"Here is on reason. "JJ grew up new Tallahassee, Florida. With the money her husband left her she bought a beach house. Of course, she traveled back and forth from Florida to Aiken. Eventually she stayed at the beach house there more than in Aiken."

"Here is the storyline. The phone rings again. This time, the invitation was to visit her at the beach for an extended weekend because she missed me."

Lisa: "You gave in to her request and visited, didn't you?"

"Bingo, you win, "I still cared deeply for her and as time went on and "D" left the scene, I was single again, I have needs to you know.

The Evil Within Them

Lisa: "I get that from your stories. Please continue."

"It is a seven-hour drive to her beach house. I can say she bought a beautiful place. But as with all the previous women. It needs some TLC from her favorite handyperson. Thus, the reason for the invitation is now clear. It was not about us reuniting or a relationship, it was about repairs.

Lisa: "You must be very handy with a hammer."

"You have no idea what I can do with a hammer."

"Do not say it, I will continue. During one trip she asked if I could install additional receptacles underneath the house. Beach house construction consists of elevated stilts to avoid flood damage. Not because it is a clever idea it is to limit insurance company losses. To accomplish this required me to intercept the wiring feeding two existing sodium lights, I had one set of receptacles installed, so I turned the circuit breaker back on and checked the power at the receptacles. Everything was on. I then checked the operation of the existing sodium lights. When I flipped the switch the lights did not work. I checked my wiring connections several times and could not get the lights to operate. I was unsure.

"It was getting later in the day and "JJ" wanted to go out for food and cocktails at a friend's house a couple of streets over. As we were leaving the house she inquired into my progress."

"The honest Abe in me prevailed, I mentioned the lights are now not working and provided a reasonable explanation as to why they may not be operational in daylight. I suggested the lights could have a built-in photocell preventing them from turning on with the remaining daylight."

Lisa rights herself in her chair and snaps her fingers in my face as she yells.

Lisa: "FIREWORKS! I am guessing she exploded on you."

231

The Evil Within Them

"Dam you are good at your job.

"We had started walking to her friend's house when I made the call to tell "JJ" my thoughts with the issue I discovered with the lights.

"I was immediately met with another verbal tirade of words that have not ben hurled at me since my time in bootcamp in the US Army."

"I was pummeled with words of being a failure, of how could I screw up her lights, you had better fix this before you leave this beach, finally I heard, those lights do not have a photocell installed in them."

"We returned to her house in the dark, the lights were not on. We went upstairs, watched a little tv and fell asleep. Th next morning while she was still in bed, I ventured downstairs under the house to work on the lights. Before going down the stairs I flipped the switch for the lights as I walked the steps down to ground level. The lights were on momentarily then switched off. Closer examination I found the photocell high above near the top of the fixture. It was so small I failed to see it in the low light of the previous evening, The switched was in the wrong position to power them."

232

The Evil Within Them

Lisa: "You did bring this to her attention didn't you?"

"Let me finish, I slowly walked back upstairs contemplating how I was going to show her. Well, "JJ" was out of bed. Come with me, we have an invitation to have mimosas on the beach at another friend's house.

Stepping off the last step, I asked her to come over to the sodium lights. I reached up with my finger covering the photocell simulating darkness. The light shined its brilliant light on us.

I said, see the lights in fact do have factory installed photocells and I wired them correctly. What do you say now?

Lisa: "Woohoo, you showed her. What did she say to you when you put your finger on it, and the light came on?"

"Absolutely nothing, she turned away to walk to the beach for her morning alcohol fix. I removed my finger and followed behind like a good boy."

The Evil Within Them

"Lisa: "Are you telling me she not once apologized for her verbal assault the evening before. No apology at all?"

"Nope, not a word from her lips. "JJ" was more concerned with her morning alcohol fix than repairing my ego." By the way, "JJ" starts every morning with a shot of Baileys in her coffee to start the flow of alcohol in her veins.""

Lisa: "Please tell me this was it? Wait, knowing you, and the history of your stories with "JJ" You went back for more abuse, didn't you?"

"Could not resist the temptation for more of the same. Correct again. But this time I discovered the other guy.

Lisa: "Michael! Why did you return?

The Evil Within Them

"Blind love for her or the constant loneliness I face every day.

Lisa: "Ok I get it, and I do not need to say it but continue."

"During this trip to visit her we went out to a local seafood restaurant. Great seafood and burgers. They actually shuck ouster right in front of you. That particular evening the guy whose job is too shuck oysters walked over to us from the employee side of the bar and stood looking at "JJ" with a concerned look on his face. I could tell he was visibly upset with her.

"That look on his face was a classic look. He was upset at my presence with her. But it was obvious to me, I had been, paraded in there to show him she was in full ownership and control of what was between her legs, and he could not do a dam thing about."

Lisa: "She was having an affair with another guy and inviting you to see him face to face. How evil of her. She knew exactly what she was doing putting the two of you face to face in the same place at the same time."

"Played me like a fiddle."

Lisa: "Played both of you."

"That she did. But the real confirmation came as we were leaving. I had stepped away to relieve the pressure of drinking. When I returned to escort her out to the car, I watched as she stepped up on the footrail leaning over the bar attempting to kiss him goodbye. His ego crushed, and he stepped back from her attempt to right a wrong situation."

Lisa: "Right in front of you. Do you think she was teaching you the same lesson of ownership?"

"I have no doubt. The weekend was over, and I left to go home. A couple of months passed and once again I get the call to return to the beach. This time she

was honest enough to instruct me to bring wood working tools to build a storage shed under stairs at her
house. Before you ask any questions I will say, No I did
not enquire if her oyster shucker was still shucking her
oyster. I loaded my tools and headed to the beach. My
thoughts were always this. I convinced myself she had
changed her ways and was now understanding something clearly at last I was the man she needed in her life.

Lisa: "You were wrong again weren't you?

"Completely wrong on all counts your honor."

"I know I continued to try with "JJ" I could not
get her off my mind. I wanted to collaborate with her.
She would push me away then reel me in like a fish
hooked in the corner of the mouth. Every night we slept
together I had to leave her bed for one reason or another.
She would either beat me with her fist, violently kick
me with her feet or curse me for turning over on my
opposite side to be comfortable."

237

The Evil Within Them

"I do know she was taking Ambien to sleep when her husband passed but whatever she was on while living at the beach was extremely worse. She had no recollection of what she did to me the night before as if her minds hard drive now scrubbed clean."

I continued to drive seven hours down to see her, she missed me and wanted to see me. Every trip I tried to convince myself she left the other man. I know this was never the case. She needed a change of pace. When she succeeded in making him mad, she called me for service, and vice versus.

"The last trip was in early November, a day or two after Halloween. Same protocol, same reasons for requesting my presence, please come down to the beach. Hesitating I eventually agreed to make the trip."

Lisa: "You mentioned this was the final trip. You came to your senses during that final trip? I have been waiting to hear the end of this story for two months now."

238

The Evil Within Them

"Well, here it comes. The end of the story.' I knew there was always a hidden reason for me to come down and stay with her.

Lisa: "I am seeing this pattern with her."

"One morning we were enjoying the sunrise and coffee and a shot of Baileys liqueur. We were happier than we have been. "JJ" started discussing the possibility of me coming down for a Thanksgiving with a few invited friends at the beach house. I was to bring food from my restaurant, and she would supply the rest. Everything was set."

"That evening we had happy hour cocktails at a friend's house a couple of doors down. I talked to the head of the household, and she talked to the head of the household. Nothing seemed out of place, we came home. Enjoyed each other romantically and fell asleep."

"Until coffee and breakfast the next morning when "JJ" asked when I was going down to help move the couch out of the same friend's house. I responded that I h informed of that request from her friend."

The Evil Within Them

Lisa put her head in her hands again and asks.

Lisa: "Oh no. No Not again. More fireworks?"

"The explosive nature of that woman shook the neighborhood. You know I have a hearing problem and the hearing aids I wear do not notice every word spoken, I miss a lot of words spoken in a group conversation."

"JJ' belittled me so terribly bad that morning. Without a word spoken to her I left her house and started down the street to help the man move the couch. She stepped out onto the landing at the top of the stairs and asked where, I was going?"

"My verbal response was brutal I had enough of her aggrieve behavior. My response to her was audible for a long way off as I let her have both barrels for criticizing my hearing disability. That was the last straw."

Returning to her house, I packed up and left. I was home when she called to talk, not to apologize as you would think. She was inquiring if I still had an interest in coming back for Thanksgiving?

240

The Evil Within Them

I informed her I would not be returning to participate in Thanksgiving. A few days later she reached out via text messaging. I finally had the courage to present detailed analysis of the last six years of her playing her game and manipulation with me, to her family and the other guy she had been sleeping with over the last six years."

It was finally over; I stood up against the,

Evil within her.

Lisa: "I am so proud of you; this is the ending I wanted to hear. Not as a therapist but as your friend. You deserve a medal for this one."

"Go home Michael and raise a glass of your favorite bourbon and rejoice to your courage. I will see you next month."

The Evil Within Them

I left Lisa's office for the first time in all the previous sessions with my head held high. For me, the future was finally opening up. The sky above me was void of clouds, if I could see heaven from my earthy position, this is how I envision it.

'I am but a mere mortal of a man, temporarily in human form. Many times, during my lifetime, I have sacrificed my personal goals for the love of others, the scars I have, my faults, beliefs, and the burdens I carry, are of my own admission, no one instills them in me. My life is in constant search for its final destination.'

The drive home is quick, I have a new soul.

The Evil Within Them

The Evil Within Them

Session Fourteen

Years have passed since my divorce. My journey now filled with joy, happiness, and sorrow. I am a stronger person now than before I began therapy. I feel empathy for the ones I walked away from. They did provide comfort during the era spanning my time with each of them, refraining from ugly direct confrontations.

I was born with a gift to forgive people for their evil actions, either directed at me or in their general behavior. I have a sixth sense to know when enough is enough. This unspoken knowledge is my key to living a successful life.

Living with a hearing disability has doomed many of my relationships with a different sex and with selective friends who do not understand the difficult challenges I face daily. They poke fun at me, intentionally speaking lower and lower to find the breaking point where I can no longer hear them, they play the "deaf card" warning friends and others of my disability, as I experience the look on their face of disbelief.

It is not a visual disability like the loss of a limb or speech impediment. No one knows the problem when they engage me for the first time. I get called vial

names behind my back because I failed to realize someone is speaking to me. Their first impression of me is, I
am an ass-hole for not responding to them.

Removing the hearing aids, shuts off the sound
of crickets, birds chirping in trees or water flowing in a
stream. I cannot experience the sound of rain falling on
my roof other than the shockwave of thunder from an
approaching storm.

These are the thoughts I process as I drive to another session with Lisa. In the quiet surroundings of her
office, I have problems conversing with her. She does
not know the difficulty she would have, engaging me in
a crowded room or listening to music in a noisier atmosphere.

I am in Columbia once again, my drive here was
the same, the walk to Lisa's office also the same, her
office with the changes she has made, is now the same.
It has become repetitious.

I enter the office door and sit in the same chair.

Lisa: "Good morning Michael. How has life
been treating you after our last session? You left with a
positive feeling of relief. I want you to know we made

considerable progress at our last meeting. Do you agree?"

I refrain from answering Lisa. She is too quick to ask a second question before I can process the first one.

Lisa: "Are we reflecting on past sessions or a new life story you need to talk about today?"

"Thank you Lisa, you have been an encouraging factor in my progress."

"I have one final person I need to discuss with you."

Lisa: "What initials are we using for this person? How did you meet her? What are the good and bad points?

"Would you prefer I jump the end of the story and save you from all the other boring details, I ask."

247

The Evil Within Them

Lisa refrains from answering, she knew she touched a nerve by starting the session with rapid questioning. She quietly sits in her chair with a lite smile forming on her face. I cannot be mad at her. She is robotic at times. Her actions are not who she really is and are not to blame for being a product of her profession. I decide to move on without her request to do so.

"Since you asked. I will refer to her as "DBR" we met at a monthly Aiken Chamber of commerce ambassador meeting. I noticed her right away. She chose a chair directly across from me. At the start of every meeting each of us in turn reports who we are and what business we are representing as ambassadors. The first meeting ended, and we were all disbursed. The next month's gathering of ambassadors she selected a chair next to mine and engaged in small talk. With every meeting we exchange our name and business profile to begin the meeting. At this meeting I had the opportunity to promote a new restaurant I was opening. Inviting everyone to attend the soft opening.

The Evil Within Them

As I was leaving the Chamber meeting, "DBR" made a point to stop me at the front door to engage in small talk. Nothing out of the ordinary we finished our talk and went about our business. That evening, I checked my email from her. It contained references to being a businessperson and she was interested in hearing my success story over dinner sometime.

Lisa: "She initiated first contact and asked you to go out with her?"

"Yes, I have mentioned they target me. I am a sucker for a pretty lady so, I agreed to meet her at my favorite Italian restaurant. From that first encounter at the chamber to the first dinner together I felt a strong connection. She was a beautiful curly redhead with a slim figure. Extremely articulate with a professional attitude for business.

"DBR" was different from the beginning. Our relationship strengthened to the point we shared the sweetest thoughts towards each other. We talked every day, we never missed an opportunity to say good morning or good night via text messages, I authored poems to her, she authored poems to me. Our feelings for each other were so strong we each expressed at one time or another to the other how we could not see living without the other one in our life. The devotion we expressed match no one before her. I found the soulmate I have been searching for my entire life. I had unconditional love for this woman.

Lisa: "I know from previous sessions not to get excited for you. So, as your therapist I have to ask. What happened?"

"Nothing."

Lisa: "B.S. Michael, I know you by now."

"Lisa, we had the best life together. We took trips out of town, we began spending the weekends together, our two dogs loved playing together. For two wonderful years we did a lot of activities together without a hitch. We played card and board games like

250

scrabble and parcheesi" I have never played games with anyone, I dated ever, unless it was a drinking game.

"I was truly "in love" with this woman and she expressed she was truly "in love" with me. Nothing fell out of place. We even shared political views and agreeing on the Covid defraud we went through as a nation."

Lisa: "I am going to ask you again, what happened?"

"Nothing, there was nothing wrong Lisa."

"For two wonderful years we had the best time together. I had no problem addressing issues around her house. I redesigned her back patio, I used my truck to pick up landscaping mulch, plants, and shrubbery. I trimmed her trees and bushes around her house, and I fixed her lawn sprinkler system. We discussed installing new lighting in her house, as a previous electrical contractor I added new lighting in the living room and over her kitchen counters including new ceiling fans. I pressure washed her house, cut down a tree, I helped her move furniture out of the house when she had her wood floors sanded. Everything we did together performed flawlessly with love.

Lisa: "Thank you Michael, I understand you have the perfect woman now, I am proud of you."

"Hold that thought, before you high five me and slap me on the back with admiration. I will now tell you how the wheels started falling off one by one."

Lisa: "I knew this was too good to be true. What happened? I know you are not in therapy because you found the Ozzi and Hariet life you always wanted."

"Sadly enough, I have to agree. You are correct again. "DBR" had one last trick up her narcissistic sleeve.

Lisa: "I am out of popcorn but please, let me here it."

252

The Evil Within Them

"One final renovation request was coming. "DBR" wanted her main bathroom remodeled. I pleaded with her, "Do not start the demolition until she has all the construction materials purchased and available or the type of project will take too long and cause major distress on both of us."

Lisa: 'She didn't listen to your advice did she?'"

"Not a single bit of my advice. She told a helper of ours to come in one day and start demolishing the existing shower tile along with the rest of the walls. We were not prepared at all. The room now demolished efficiently, but we did not have replacement tiles, a toilet, a sink, or a door. Everything she wanted to use was still in an online cart that she deleted and replaced for one dumb reason or another.

"DBR" relentlessly changed her mind on every item we needed to install. The job turned into a nightmare. She took it upon herself to be the self-proclaimed construction manager, refusing to listen to advice from everyone working on the project. "DBR displayed an aggressive behavior I refused to believe she was

253

capable of. Her attitude was, "it is her house," and she was doing whatever, however she wanted, and I had no say so in the process."

Lisa: "Michael it was her house. You do not agree with her thinking on that?"

"That is the problem I did agree with her, but as soon as I agreed with her on a toilet, a sink, or the tile, even the door to the bathroom, she would purposefully change he mind. It took six months to complete the eight feet bathroom by eighteen feet."

Lisa: "Did you two fight over the schedule?"

'No, we never engaged in a verbal fight with each other over any difference in our opinions. I told you I just get quiet; I see no need in aggressive behavior as an adult. We made a pact when we first got together to calmly work things out any difference between us."

254

The Evil Within Them

Lisa: "What are your thoughts to why she became aggressive?"

"She had a plan in the woks behind the scenes. An individual's true nature will inevitably be disclosed.

Lisa: "I am listening, details please."

"I always take the time to analyze what happened after a break-up. I need this to learn from my mistakes, trying desperately to not repeat history. But this woman was the sneakiest narcissist I had the pleasure to meet."

"You see, I discovered she cheated on her first husband, and her second husband that she was still married to."

Lisa: "WHAT!" Is she still married to her second husband? Did you not know this when you were dating?"

The Evil Within Them

"Yes I knew it, we discussed it in detail. It made sense for her to stay married for the health benefits she needed, "DBR was a hypochondriac, taking multiple supplements daily. She always claimed she was sick with something.

One weekend I arrived at her house. The usual loving embrace of a hug and kisses when I arrived. I noticed an extraordinarily strong odor of dead fish emanating from her curly red hair. It was so repulsive I had to ask her what it was. She claimed she had no sense of smell and did not detect any odd odor.

It took a couple of days of discovery and eventually revealed she reached for a bottle of castor oil from her fridge to give her hair vitality. Claiming it had been falling out of her scalp in clumps in the new shower. What she inadvertently took out of the fridge was cod liver oil. It has no pungent odor until it hits the warm air after refrigeration."

I have no doubt she did this on purpose to start degrading our relationship.

Lisa: "Did you stay that weekend or go back home?"

The Evil Within Them

"Like a good Boyfriend I stayed, although the dead fish kept me awake all night."

Lisa: "Michael. You put up with a lot of crap from women."

"Indeed, I do. But that did not do the trick of running me off. She then launched an aggressive campaign against everything I had been doing right to this point was now all wrong, leaving no stone turned letting me know. I could not play scrabble or cook properly, and I was a highly regarded chef at my new restaurant.

"Nothing was working to get me to break up with her to implement the plan she had in reserve. So, "DBR" had one final card to play she knew would not fail in getting me to break up with her. That is what she needed to save face in the community."

Lisa: "What was the las card she played, Michael?"

257

The Evil Within Them

"This is hard for me Lisa; I may get emotional. I love this women mor than ice-cream, and I love ice-cream. She decided it was time to press the issue of religion. Out of all the positive reinforcing, the working together on her house renovations. After two and a half years of love, she decided we could no longer spend weekends together, have morning coffee, or share her bed. In discovery at my house, she already removed her garments from the drawers of the dresser drawer she used, her toiletries were gone. She was now implementing her plan.

Lisa: "You had differences in religious beliefs? I fail to see how you could not work that out between the two of you. I have several clients that have different beliefs."

Efforts were made to include discussions about religion, noting the absence of a religious upbringing. My parents never attended church. So, it would take time to change my thoughts on the subject."

The Evil Within Them

"To no avail, this did not move the needle. Her Plan was in full swing and nothing was going to get in her way, including me."

Lisa: "I am dying to know the plan. Please tell me what it was she was hiding from you."

"A year ago, her daughter and son-in-law moved from Pennsylvania to Arizona. They absolutely loved it out there. They moved because the son-in-law had allergies, and the climate has helped him. So, "DBR" and her hypochondriac lifestyle decided to move herself across the country without discussing the plan with me. She packed up her household and moved to Arizona.

Lisa: "I understand the move but why did she not tell you? Further why did this upset you so terribly bad?"

"The plan was to use me for the renovations, then create a diversion to get me to be the one to initiate an exit from the relationship to save her ego, while using the ruse, we were spiritually unmatched. She gaslighted everyone, including me into believing her story that our difference in religious beliefs destroyed our relationship after two solid years of telling every person and girlfriend we were a perfect match for each other."

"This was her plan all along, to fallow her daughter and son-in-law to Arizona, at any and all cost to our relationship."

"She has no empathy for what she did or the damage she caused to my emotional wellbeing, I admit I was deeply depressed, the emotional scar she left behind sent me into a rabbit hole I did not think I would ever see in my lifetime. With the culmination of all the other evil deeds bestowed on me from women the before her, I had to call the Veterans crisis line for help. I had lost control of my emotions and considered ending my life.

I was standing at the edge, considering the last step. I was kneeling in my living room and asked for a sign. At that moment, a bright light engulfed me. As quickly as it came the light disappeared, I now know he exists. He turned me around to walk a different path.

"DBR" gave me everything I had ever wanted in a relationship, and I nearly lost everything in the end."

"Lisa, please "DO NOT" try to convince me this woman "did not" possess an "EVIL WITHIN HER."

Lisa: "After listening to you today. I do not think I could ever say that to you Michael." How are you feeling now that you have expressed your feelings during these sessions with me, do you have any resentment towards these women you shared during our sessions?"

"I harbor no ill feelings; it is who I am. It is my forgiving them for their actions that make me a stronger, better person than they have become.

The Evil Within Them

My only hope is you can use the recordings to help others, I know there are other people who have had similar experiences.

Hopefully, they choose the right path.

I leave you now Lisa, I have finished my story.

Lisa has tears in her eyes as she says goodbye to me. I now embark on one last trip back to Aiken in search of a meaningful relationship once again.

The Evil Within Them

The Evil Within Them

The Evil Within Them

I dedicate this book to everyone seeking an-swers to problematic relationships that defy normality. The brain of a narcissist does not function the same as a normally developed brain. You cannot reason with a narcissist or understand their behavior. You are merely their source and become a victim to them.

Evil Within Them.

The only option you have is to find a way out of the relationship before it destroys you.

www.ingramcontent.com/pod-product-compliance
Lightning Source LLC
Chambersburg PA
CBHW071717120626
46550CB00001B/274